# ON HER WAY

*The Life and Music of*
Shania Twain

# ON HER WAY

## The Life and Music of
## Shania Twain

### Barbara Hager

BERKLEY BOULEVARD BOOKS, NEW YORK

ON HER WAY: THE LIFE AND MUSIC OF SHANIA TWAIN

A Berkley Boulevard Book / published by arrangement with
the author

PRINTING HISTORY
Berkley Boulevard trade paperback edition / December 1998

The Penguin Putnam Inc. World Wide Web site address is
http://www.penguinputnam.com

ISBN: 0-425-16451-9

BERKLEY BOULEVARD
Berkley Boulevard Books are published by The Berkley Publishing Group,
a member of Penguin Putnam Inc., 375 Hudson Street,
New York, New York 10014.
BERKLEY BOULEVARD and its logo
are trademarks belonging to Berkley Publishing Corporation.

PRINTED IN THE UNITED STATES OF AMERICA

10 9 8 7 6 5 4 3 2 1

*Dedicated to my mother, Judy Todd, whose life was filled with music*

# CONTENTS

viii                    *Contents*

TEN
The Road Ahead   146

# ACKNOWLEDGMENTS

First and foremost, I would like to thank my family, Lee, Sarah and Jordyn, who have once again displayed great patience, love and support while I was in the "book zone." I'd also like to thank Olive Hager for her warm support over the years.

My sincere thanks to my agents Carolyn Swayze and Jeff Gerecke (JCA), for finding such a great publishing team to take on this book. Special thanks to my editor at Berkley, Elizabeth Beier, for her talent and contagious enthusiasm and for giving me the time I needed. I'd also like to thank Barry Neville, Ginjer Buchanan and Jessa Stephens at Berkley and Design Monsters for their help with my book.

My appreciation to Dave Spavin and his staff at Victoria Travel Shoppe, for making sure that I always arrived in the right city at the right time for my interviews, and for finding me the hotel with the guitar-shaped swimming pool in Nashville.

I'd like to thank Paul Peters for all the coffee, and for his country music resources; Mary Truscott for being my closest long-distance friend and literary critic; Cindy Carleton, a fellow working mother who came to my rescue when I needed more time to write; Greg Claeys for his warm support and for being my two-step partner; Don Colborne for his astute legal advice; and April Butler, who was always there when I desperately needed a fact checked or a good friend to talk to.

Finally, I would like to thank David Malachowski, the only musician I have ever met who excels in the dual roles of music journalist and guitarist extraordinaire. His involvement in this book was invaluable, and I cannot thank him enough for his insights and his collaboration on the chapter "The Power of Music."

# INTRODUCTION

The radios of my childhood were always set to country and western music. On summer evenings, we would all pile into my stepfather's pine green Delta 88 and cruise down Highway 1, the dry summer air flowing crazily through the car. In the front seat, my mother and stepfather would alternate singing (loudly) along with songs on the radio— Merle Haggard, Dolly Parton, Charley Pride, Loretta Lynn. There was never much conversation on those drives, just the unabashed belting out of country hits into the waning summer evening. They seemed oblivious to everything around them—kids squabbling in the backseat, peculiar stares from passing motorists, pleas to stop for a rest room break. Sometimes I would learn a line or two of the latest country hit and in a voice so low it went undetected, I would sing along with them from the backseat.

What I remember so distinctly from that time in my life,

when I was twelve years old and had no comprehension of love and relationships, is how unbearably sad those country and western songs all seemed to be. Someone was always cheating, or leaving, or losing or lying. I came to the conclusion that if this is what I had to look forward to in adult life, I didn't want to ever grow up.

When my mother left my stepfather, and packed up all our things and moved us west to start a fresh life, I remember thinking that my mother's *life* could be a country song. It seemed that every time I listened to country and western music on the radio I would catch glimpses of my mother's poignant life, and sometimes I found myself crying along with the radio.

A few years ago, I was driving down the highway, flipping through radio stations, when I came across a local country station. I listened to a few songs, and was amazed to discover that country music isn't that hard-luck, cry-in-your-beer, stand-by-your-man music that I used to listen to, somewhat reluctantly, on those family drives. The music I was hearing was still melodramatic, but there was a rich musical diversity that seemed unfamiliar. Even though the songs eagerly included traditional country instruments like steel guitars, fiddles and harmonicas, they often featured the driving sound of rock or the jauntiness of pop music. The familiar twang of traditional country vocals hadn't been completely buried, but they were tempered by singers who sounded downright urban. And the lyrics were clever, more often about life changes than life crises.

As a teenager, I had sworn off country and western as music for married couples, cowboys and old folks, and I wasn't about to rush back in. At first, I didn't want to make a commitment. I listened to country music on the radio and on country music video stations, but I was reluctant to buy CDs by country artists. After all, that would be admitting that I actually *liked* the music my parents listened to.

Then, in March 1995, I went to an awards ceremony at the Queen Elizabeth Theater in Vancouver, British Columbia, and one of the performers was a virtually unknown Canadian country singer. She sang a rollicking, irreverent song about "what every woman wants." The initial response from the black-tie crowd, after they'd recovered from their surprise over this captivating country singer with an attitude, was to tap their toes and smile. The next day I went out and bought *The Woman in Me* CD by Shania Twain. I had come home to country music, and I was pretty darn sure that I was not alone.

That was more than three years ago, and since that time *The Woman in Me* has sold over thirteen million copies worldwide, making it the biggest-selling album by a country female artist in history, even surpassing the numbers of the legendary Patsy Cline. Shania's third platinum-mine CD, *Come on Over*, has firmly entrenched her in the music industry history books, and further endeared her to millions of fans worldwide.

In 1996, I met Shania Twain in Los Angeles, the day before she performed at the Academy of Country Music Awards at the Universal Amphitheater. Twain had agreed to be interviewed for my book *Honor Song: A Tribute* (Raincoast Books, 1996), which profiles sixteen leading Aboriginal Canadians. Her chapter in *Honor Song* was based on my interview with her in L.A., another earlier telephone interview and extensive research into her musical history.

I made the decision to write a full-length music biography of Shania Twain soon after my first book was published. Shania was making music history, and I wanted to document this significant and exciting phase in her career. As a music journalist and biographer, I believe that the inside story of Shania's life and music is one that her fans desire and deserve.

While I was doing research for this book, I interviewed dozens of people who have played a role in Shania's music career at some point in the past twenty-five years. I discovered that there are few people who have not fallen under the spell of her musical gifts or who have been unaffected by her genuineness and charm.

I am greatly indebted to the men and women who have helped me tell the story of Shania's music career, from her childhood in Timmins to her meteoric rise in the world of country music. Without their support, this book would not have been possible.

I hope that you will find *On Her Way: The Life and Music of Shania Twain* to be a book that is as compelling, spirited and spontaneous as the singer herself.

CHAPTER ONE

# FROM BARN DANCE TO NEW COUNTRY

*The crowd in the smoke-filled lounge at the Mattagami Hotel has thinned out, and the waitresses, eager to head home after a long night of serving rum and Cokes and draft beer, are busily wiping off tables and straightening out chairs. The four-piece country band has put on a good show, but the dance floor is empty now and the musicians have left the stage. They are either sitting around talking with friends who have stayed on after last call or having a cigarette outside in the cool northern Canadian air.*

*One of the waitresses calls out across the nearly empty club, "Hey, boys, get back up there and make some music—the little Twain girl is here." The bass player walks across the room and greets a couple who have just entered the club. With them is a child no more than eight years old, oddly out of place at this late hour of the night. The girl's father offers the bass player a hearty handshake and her mother walks with her over to the guitar player, who is sitting at the bar chatting with the bartender as*

*she cleans up for the night. The brown-haired child seems sur-
prisingly oblivious to the smell of spilled beer and cigarettes that
fills the air.*

*"Come on, Bob, stop flirting and get up there onstage again,"
the girl's mother says affectionately to the guitarist. She takes
her daughter's coat from her and hands her the wooden acoustic
guitar she has carried into the bar. The instrument is almost as
tall as the girl, and her mother helps her place the leather strap
over her shoulder.*

*Bob tousles the little girl's hair. "Wake up there, Eilleen. We
worked up that Parton song just for you," he says to her. The
girl smiles, suddenly wide awake and eager to try out the song
that she's been hearing all week on the radio.*

*"I learned all the words to 'Jolene,'" she says shyly, "but my
uncle hasn't taught me all the chords yet."*

*The band slowly regroups and steps back up to the stage—
four seasoned musicians, all somewhat amused and in awe of this
half-pint singer who is standing patiently at the microphone, her
oversized guitar cradled awkwardly in her small arms. The lead
guitarist counts one-two-three-four, and in that moment before
the rhythm section swings into the song, Eilleen looks out into
the thinning audience for the reassuring faces of her parents.
Then she begins to sing.*

◆　　◆　　◆

Eilleen Regina Twain was eight years old when she began singing and playing the guitar in public. Her parents,
Jerry and Sharon Twain, were fervent country music fans.
It was the music that Eilleen heard every day at home, and
it naturally became the music she performed. Her parents

would sometimes wake her up after midnight and take her to sing with the country band in the lounge of the Mattagami Hotel in Timmins, Ontario, after the bar had closed and it was no longer illegal for a minor to be in the club. In those early years of Twain's music career, she was as familiar with the music of Dolly Parton, Tammy Wynette and Waylon Jennings as most children her age are with Mother Goose songs.

The music that the Twains were so crazy about would eventually lead Eilleen—who would change her name to Shania in the early 1990s—down the path to a phenomenally successful country music career.

But to truly appreciate the music that Eilleen was "born into" and performed as a young musician, you need to reach back to the early roots of country music. Back through time, through the layers of styles that have defined the music—New Country, Country Rock, Urban Cowboy, Outlaw Country, the Nashville Sound, Honky-tonk, the Grand Ole Opry, Cowboy Music, Western Swing, Bluegrass and Rural Folk.

When Eilleen began performing country music as a child, and later when she began a country recording career, she became part of a rich musical heritage that traces its history back to the mid-1920s and which counts among its luminaries some of the biggest names in the history of American music.

The first fifty years of country music were largely a man's world—dominated by male producers, writers, musicians and recording artists. Women were more of an anomaly, with only a handful enjoying successful recording careers during that period. Though they were few and far between, Sara Carter, Kitty Wells, Patsy Montana, Patsy Cline and a few others had a profound impact on the generation of women singers to follow them. Eilleen's musical role model, Dolly Parton, and her contemporaries Loretta Lynn, Tammy Wynette and Lynn Anderson carried the torch from the 1960s to the 1980s, when they handed it off to Reba McEntire, the Judds, Emmylou Harris, Tanya Tucker and other musically independent women.

All of these influential women singers, musicians and songwriters were like shooting stars lighting up a universe crowded by men. They were a rich legacy to draw upon for all those young women in the 1990s who were looking for their own distinct brand of country.

Through all the incarnations and style shifts that country music has been through since the 1920s, there remains one universal truth—it has always been the music that has talked to the heart and soul of rural and small-town America. Even so, country fans have never shut the door on their city cousins who stop in, every generation or so, for a listen. In the late 1970s, the movie soundtrack of the hit Hollywood movie *Urban Cowboy* briefly brought country music to the metropolitan masses, and in the 1990s, new country has attracted an increasingly urban, baby-boomer audience.

Popular music today, in all its distinguished genres, had its auspicious start in 1876 when the phonograph was invented. By 1900, the magical sound of a 78 playing on a Victrola—a newfangled machine made by RCA Victor—could be heard in homes across the country.

In 1915, the earliest whisper of the coming-rural-music revolution came with the recording of the first fiddle-driven folk songs. By the early 1920s, the first country "stars" were emerging. Texan Eck Robertson is credited, in 1922, as being the first "country" artist, and three years later, Vernon Dalhart scored with the first million-selling country record, "The Prisoner Song" and "The Wreck of the Old '97."

Back in those days, there was no such thing as a record store, or even a mail-order club offering ten records for a dollar. Recordings were sold through department stores, such as Sears Roebuck and Montgomery Ward.

Even in the infancy of country music, album covers with appealing photographs and liner notes were important tools in attracting fans. In the mid-1920s, two recording groups emerged that featured women musicians and singers in their ensembles. The Dixie Mountaineers, put together by musician/songwriter Ernest Stoneman, included his wife, Hattie, on fiddle. The Carter Family, led by the domineering patriarch A. P., included his wife, Maybelle, on harmonica and guitar, and her cousin Sara, who became country's first female star.

While country music was emerging as a distinct genre, radio was taking its initial tentative steps as a mass communications tool in America. The first commercial radio station, KDKA, went on the air in Pittsburgh in 1920. In 1922 there were 30 radio stations across the country; the following year there were 556.

It was radio that brought country music to a vast national audience. Before radio, the only way for musicians and bands to connect "live" with their fans was to load up the car and hit the road, traveling an endless circuit of county fairs, concert halls and nightclubs. With the advent of radio, country music spread across America like a fire on the prairie. From its earliest days, radio has had the power to create superstars almost overnight. To this day, the success or failure of a song is measured in large part by its rotations—the frequency that it is played—on radio stations. A number one radio hit has an extraordinary impact on album sales, far more than concert tours or media appearances can claim.

In 1924, WLS Chicago went on the air with the National Barn Dance. The program ran for more than twenty years, and counts Patsy Montana on its alumni list. A year after the National Barn Dance was launched, WSM Nashville introduced the Grand Ole Opry, a weekly jamboree of live music that has become country music's longest-running radio show. From 1943 to 1974 the Grand Ole Opry was aired from the Ryman Auditorium in Nashville. The Ryman was abandoned for Opryland, a posh mega-entertainment complex in Nashville. The Ryman, however, was recently restored by historic preservationists, and it is once again an active concert hall.

For decades, becoming a member of the Grand Ole Opry was one of the most coveted "musical gigs" a musician could aspire to. The show has launched a hundred careers, most notably those of Loretta Lynn, Dolly Parton, Tex Ritter, Roy Acuff, Porter Wagner and Chet Atkins.

The 1930s and 1940s saw the emergence of one of country music's most widely recognized icons—the cowboy hat—and the musical era that it is associated with. Cowboy hats define the singer who wears one. An outlaw wears black, a purist wears white. A somewhat worn hat suggests a rural or western background. It's believed that some male musicians may even use it to cover up a receding hairline. Whatever the reason, the cowboy hat remains the most recognizable symbol of country music.

The Cowboy Music era in country music was fueled by the silver screen. Country music even picked up the "western" moniker during this era, which lasted from the late 1930s through the early 1950s. The men and women most often identified with this era are among the best-loved country stars, including Patsy Montana and the Prairie Ramblers, Gene Autry, Roy Rogers and Dale Evans. It could even be argued that Gene, Roy and Dale were the first "video" stars of country music. Their crossover into film and television offered them a trail to their fans that few other artists enjoyed.

Down the road from country music live big band, Dixieland jazz and swing. Western Swing, which borrowed elements from these other styles, had its beginnings in the Texas-Oklahoma region, and existed almost solely as dance music. With the Great Depression as its backdrop, Western Swing must have seemed like a vaudeville act at a funeral. Its sound was big, often performed by eighteen- to twenty-piece bands, and it was pure escape music. Bob Wills, a fiddler from Texas, was at the forefront of this jaunty country style, which was prominent until World War II.

A cousin to country music, Bluegrass was popularized in the late 1930s and 1940s by the string-band group Bill Monroe's Blue Grass Boys. This acoustic style features two-part vocal harmonies, and instrumentation that includes banjo, mandolin, fiddle, guitar and bass. Bluegrass enjoyed a revival in the 1960s in grassroot university settings, and today is a staple of regional festivals and country fairs.

Honky-tonk was the brash, post–World War II party music of the 1940s and 1950s. Featuring electric and pedal steel guitars, and typically delivered by live bands or juke-boxes in smoky bars, Honky-tonk's socially reckless attitude was a contrast to the more respectable themes of traditional country music. Some of the Honky-tonk greats include Lefty Frizzell, George Jones, Ernest Tubb and Hank Williams.

In the 1950s, country music began experimenting with other popular music forms, which many artists borrowed from to create a smooth, pop-oriented style that became known as the Nashville Sound. The rise of this style coincided with the growing preeminence of Nashville as the capital of country music and with the success of many of the artists who were living and recording there, often utilizing Nashville-based songwriters and producers.

It was the decade of teen music, bobby sox and Elvis Presley. Presley got his start as a country crooner, opening for acts like Hank Snow and Faron Young. In 1955, he was featured in *Country Song Roundup* magazine. Presley was named "Most Promising New Country and Western Artist" at the 1954 Deejay Convention in Nashville. There were those in the country music industry who felt that Presley was too "R&B" to be a country star. It wasn't long, however, before Presley got swept away from country to the emerging world of pop and rock 'n' roll, where he achieved phenomenal success. Although he abandoned country music for greener pastures, he did teach Nashville an important message: Reach out and capture the teenage market, or lose it for good.

At about the same time that Presley was charting his first

hit, Patsy Cline was emerging as a formidable talent. Cline, who epitomized the Nashville Sound, got her break in 1957 when she was a winner on *Arthur Godfrey's Talent Scouts* singing "Walking After Midnight." Signed to the Decca label, she continued to produce hit after hit, including the classic "I Fall to Pieces." Both Cline and Jim Reeves, another prominent Nashville Sound founder, died in plane crashes at the peak of their music careers in the early 1960s. Years after their deaths, the wizardry of sound editing resulted in two spliced-together duets by Cline and Reeves— "Have You Ever Been Lonely?" and "I Fall to Pieces."

Decca released *Patsy Cline's Greatest Hits* in 1967, and it went on to become the biggest-selling album by a female country artist ever, until Shania Twain eclipsed it with her 1995 release *The Woman in Me.*

By the early 1960s, the Nashville Sound dominated the radio airwaves and was attracting an expanding audience. The country audience, which had lost a large percentage of its real and potential audience in the 1950s to pop and rock, began to regain ground. In 1961, there were eighty full-time country stations in the United States; by the end of the decade, there were over five hundred.

The 1960s, however, were a tumultuous decade for America, and country music did not escape the turmoil that was sweeping the country. The Vietnam War, the sexual revolution, drugs and the Kennedy and King assassinations shattered the carefree, prosperous postwar 1950s. A return to traditional country values mixed with a dark, renegade style, known as Outlaw Country, emerged in the 1960s, led by Willie Nelson, Johnny Cash, Merle Haggard and Charley Pride.

The Outlaws gave way to the Urban Cowboys, an infamous, short-lived era in the late 1970s that saw a radical shift away from the roots of country. This hybrid of pop culture and country was fueled by the success of two Hollywood movies—*9 to 5*, starring Dolly Parton, and *Urban Cowboy*, starring John Travolta. An easy-listening crossover sound, Urban Cowboy music was capitalized by Janie Fricke, John Conlee, Alabama and Reba McEntire. Another crossover music trend from that time period was Country Rock, which created major careers for Emmylou Harris, Linda Ronstadt, Glen Campbell, Kris Kristofferson, Willie Nelson, Hank Williams Jr. and Waylon Jennings.

It is not surprising that country fans, overexposed to the darker, grittier themes of Outlaw Country, eagerly embraced a new generation of confident and witty female artists in the 1970s. The women in this era were strong and self-assured, a reflection of the way that women were asserting themselves in all areas of society. Suddenly, women were being taken seriously in the recording studio and in the radio industry. Loretta Lynn, Dolly Parton, Tanya Tucker and Tammy Wynette were unquestionably country and feminine, but they were not afraid to take on a tough social issue or to stand up for what they believed in.

By the mid-1980s, country music was facing its worst nightmare. Its fan base was shrinking, and the average age of its audience was reported to be close to fifty years old. The Urban Cowboy cycle had fizzled out, and there was no heir apparent waiting in the wings to usher in the next era—until New Traditionalist Randy Travis arrived on the scene. Young, attractive and earnest, he had one foot planted in country music's past, and one in its future. His songs were authentic and pure, and he represented a new beginning for an ailing music industry. The prototype male wunderkind was created, and it turned out that there were talented young musicians and singers in almost every state south of the Mason-Dixon Line, working the regional country music circuits with the dream of someday making it in Nashville. Some of the standouts in this crop of recording artists include Brooks and Dunn, Vince Gill, Alan Jackson, John Michael Montgomery, George Strait, Marty Stuart and Dwight Yoakam. It was this era that produced the formidable Garth Brooks, the biggest-selling male country star in history, with close to sixty-five million record sales to his credit.

The rise of the superstar created the need for outlets for the superfan. Since 1972, promoters have been holding an annual Fan Fair in Nashville. Fans get to realize the fantasy of meeting their favorite artists, and record labels get to strut their roster of artists to an ultraloyal group of country music record consumers. In the past decade, the event has grown into the biggest country music party of the year. Held every year in June in Nashville, Fan Fair regularly sells out its 24,000 tickets. Besides this annual pilgrimage to Nashville, fans can keep informed by joining fan clubs, some of which have helped artists reach cult status.

The new wave of male country stars discovered quickly that there was some fierce competition for airplay, video rotation and fans. An entire generation of young, talented and photogenic women singers were taking the country music world by storm. Strongly influenced by the confident and assertive musical style of their older sisters, Loretta, Dolly, Tammy and Reba, they were not only capable of winning the country fan, but also appealed to the pop and Country Rock audience. In 1996, for the first time in the history of country music, women artists sold as many records in the United States as their male counterparts. Even more important to Nashville's record labels, women artists were being embraced by urban baby boomers—the dream demographic of retailers in North America.

The trend, which began in the late 1980s and has not slowed down, may not yet have a moniker, like so many of its predecessors, but "the Female Invasion" might be apt. And with the fierce individualism and distinct country style that characterize each and every one of these singers, there seems to be little risk of the genre becoming stale and redundant anytime soon. This era has produced some of the most recognizable women in recent history—the Judds, Tanya Tucker, Pam Tillis, Trisha Yearwood, Kathy Mattea, Patty Loveless, Terry Clark, Faith Hill, LeAnn Rimes and Mary Chapin Carpenter.

The latest chapter in the rich and dynamic history of country music belongs to Shania Twain. In 1996, on the strength of her second CD, *The Woman in Me*, Shania became the biggest-selling female artist in the seventy-five-year history of country music. She achieved this extraordinary feat without the benefit of a live tour, but instead by relying on the musical power of forty-five minutes of music, eight music videos and a handful of televised and live performances.

As with all the remarkably talented female recording artists who came before her—Carter, Wells, Montana, Cline, Lynn, Parton, Wynette, McEntire and many many more—the story of Shania's musical career has already become an integral part of the story of country music.

Country music has proven, time and time again, to be a genre that is continually reinventing itself, reviving its best attributes and adding influences from other musical genres. As the story of Shania Twain's musical history is revealed in the chapters to follow, it will become evident that she, like all of the musical giants who preceded her, is as much a part of country music as country music is a part of her.

## CHAPTER TWO

# THE NORTHERN YEARS

*Outside Eilleen's bedroom window, a bitter eastern wind is lifting the dry snow and spinning it into eddies of whiteness. After spending most of the afternoon ice-skating at the outdoor rink at the community center, Eilleen's fingers are still too numb to play the wire strings on her acoustic guitar. She holds her hands over the warm air that's blowing from the furnace grate on her bedroom floor.*

*From the living room downstairs, she can hear the sound of Al Cherny playing fiddle on* The Tommy Hunter Show. *Her parents watch the show religiously every week, but lately, Eilleen has been more interested in the music she's been hearing on stations from Toronto and Detroit that she can pick up on clear nights on her transistor radio. Country and western has always been the music that's filled the Twain house, but when she's alone in her room, Eilleen has her radio tuned to Top 40 stations.*

*"We had a request earlier tonight from Eilleen in Timmins*

*for anything by the Carpenters," she hears the DJ on the local pop station say just as she tunes in. "We'll go back to 1970 with 'We've Only Just Begun.' This one's for you, Eilleen."*

*Eilleen turns up the volume and closes her eyes to listen. There probably isn't another singer, other than Dolly, that she loves more than Karen Carpenter. She picks up her guitar and begins strumming quietly along with the song on the radio, her fingertips still a bit stiff from being outside in the frigid air all afternoon.*

*"Eilleen," her mother calls to her from the living room, "it's time to turn out the lights."*

*"Just one more song, Mom," she calls back.*

*When the song ends, Eilleen rests her guitar against the wall and climbs under the covers. She reaches for her radio and slips it underneath the blankets with her, the Supremes still singing their latest hit as she falls into a deep, dreamless sleep.*

◆　　◆　　◆

Eilleen Regina Twain was born on August 28, 1965, in Windsor, Ontario, but she lived most of her childhood and teenage years in Timmins, a bustling mining center in northern Ontario with a population today of about 47,000.

For Eilleen, life growing up in northern Canada was not much different from that of other girls her age during the 1970s: After school she had her daily chores, probably some homework assignments and then a couple hours watching popular TV shows like *The Brady Bunch* or *Charlie's Angels* or *The Waltons*. But for Eilleen, evenings and weekends offered an alternative—practicing the guitar or writing songs. She was ten years old when she first started penning her own songs, even though she admits today that she was too young to really comprehend the things she was writing about. She modeled her songs after the music that her parents played on the radio or on the eight-track player in their truck—melodramatic themes like losing at love or leaving someone behind that are so common in country music.

Eilleen's first memories of music go back much further. When she was three years old she would find a quiet hiding place in her house, and she'd sing a song like "Twinkle, Twinkle, Little Star," changing the rhythm and humming different tones. She didn't know it at the time, but her mother, Sharon, was listening to her daughter's early musical experimentation. By the time Eilleen was in grade school, her mother and father had bought her a guitar and were guiding her toward the stage. One of her first "public" performances came when she was in first grade: Eilleen sang John Denver's "Country Roads" during show-and-tell. She claims that the performance didn't go over well with her classmates, and she felt they all considered her a "show-off." For years afterward, she had stage fright, which apparently was rooted in that first, critical audience of five- and six-year-olds at school.

It didn't take too many years before Sharon found the perfect place for Eilleen to perform. Wearing stage outfits made by Eilleen's grandmother, her mother would take her to the seniors' home where her great-grandfather Twain lived. And Sharon made sure that Eilleen was signed up to sing country songs and play her guitar whenever there was a community fair, holiday festival or local telethon.

When she was just starting out, Eilleen's stepfather,

Jerry, who played a little guitar, taught her a few chords. Some of the first songs she learned on the guitar were by Canadian country legend Stompin' Tom Connors, because those were the songs her father knew. It wasn't long before she was playing in a band with some of her father's cousins and her uncle. The band performed at family gatherings, usually in the Aboriginal community where her father's family lived.

In Canadian towns such as Timmins, it doesn't take long for a talented child like Eilleen to be treated a bit differently than other children. She soon became known as the "Twain Girl," a name spoken with a certain kind of admiration for her talents as a musician and singer, and in a tone that said, "That girl is *going* somewhere."

Her mother assumed the role of primary stage parent. There wasn't always an abundance of money in the Twain household, and Eilleen's father had to be pragmatic about when and where she could perform. He would try to explain to his wife that it didn't make sense to spend money on gas to drive to a distant town to perform for free when they had to pay the heating bill that week. Eilleen recalls an instance in which her father decided that they couldn't afford to travel out of town to perform. After Eilleen went to bed that night, she crawled out of her bedroom window to where her mother was waiting, and the two went and did the show anyway. Music, Eilleen learned from an early age, was worth taking risks for.

One particular incident when Eilleen was in fifth grade illustrates how seriously she and her parents took her career. Her teacher had heard about her musical talent, and asked Eilleen to sing and play her guitar at a special parents' event at the school. Eilleen asked the teacher to call her mother to make sure she wasn't already booked somewhere else that day. Then she matter-of-factly asked the teacher if there would be a sound system and monitor for her to play through. The teacher was speechless, realizing that he wasn't talking to a student, he was negotiating with a professional musician.

Music was never seen as a hobby by Eilleen or her parents. After she began performing in public, she had a set list of songs and costumes. Her mother helped her create dialogue for the stage. Nowhere was this training put to better use than at the musical talent contests that Eilleen would compete in.

When she was nine, the Twains were living in Sudbury, Ontario, and Sharon and Jerry took Eilleen to the Sudbury Native Friendship Centre to compete in a talent contest. Another aspiring singer-songwriter, Lawrence Martin, was also competing at that contest. Lawrence, whose mother was Irish like Sharon and whose father was Cree, made a strong impression on the Twains. He was ten years older than Eilleen, and to Sharon and Jerry he was just the musical mentor their daughter needed.

A couple weeks after the Sudbury contest, Jerry, Sharon, Eilleen, Lawrence and his girlfriend, Connie, who would later become his wife, drove out to Brandon, Manitoba, for an Aboriginal talent contest. They left on a Thursday afternoon and drove all night, arriving in Brandon, which was over a thousand miles away, the following evening, just an hour before the contest was to begin. Exhausted and cramped from having just spent over twenty-four hours in a car, Eilleen and Lawrence got up onstage and competed

as both solo vocalists and as a duo. To everyone's aston-
ishment, they won in all three categories.

Over the next few years, Lawrence and Eilleen often performed as a duo at concerts, talent shows and Christmas
events. Sometimes Eilleen's cousin Kenny Derasp would
join them on guitar. Lawrence recalls that he would go over
to the Twains' house and they'd all watch music specials
on television, studying every stage and musical move the
performers would make. Then he and Eilleen would sit
around talking about how they could improve their performances.

Lawrence recalls that his first impression of Eilleen was
that the little girl—whose guitar was almost as big as she
was—had the kind of talent that would take her to the top
of the music business. His prediction, not surprising to
him, proved right, although he's surprised it took her until
her late twenties to get recognized, considering that the
talent was there when she was just a very young girl.

Lawrence and the Twains fell out of touch when he
moved to Moosonee, Ontario, his family's hometown, in
1978. Later, Lawrence had a successful career in television
broadcasting, became a Juno Award–winning recording
artist (under the Cree name Wapistan, on the First Nations
Music label) and served as the mayor of Moose Factory,
Ontario. Though they haven't been in touch in years, Eilleen considers Lawrence to be the first musician, outside
of her family, to have treated her like a serious singer-
songwriter.

A few years later, when she was barely in her teens,
Eilleen performed on the popular Canadian country variety
program *The Tommy Hunter Show*. (Ronnie Milsap and Glen

Campbell performed on the same shows that she was on.) This popular weekly country music variety show ran from 1965 to 1992 on CBC-TV, and featured both emerging as well as top Canadian and American country acts. For an up-and-coming country singer like Eilleen, *The Tommy Hunter Show* represented the single most important performance of a young career. She also had guest appearances on the Canadian television shows *Opry North, Easy Country* and *The Mercey Brothers Show*.

Eilleen also played the country music circuit in Ontario, and on more than one occasion she crossed paths with a Canadian country singer named Mary Bailey.

Mary and Eilleen met in 1978 when Eilleen, then twelve years old, was an opening act for a concert that Mary was headlining in Sudbury. Mary was backstage and heard Eilleen sing Hank Williams's "I'm So Lonesome I Could Cry." The performance was so poignant that it brought tears to Mary's eyes. She introduced herself to Sharon and told her how impressed she was by Eilleen. Perhaps she was flashing back to her own youth, when she had been a country music child prodigy. Her parents had started her out singing publicly when she was five, but by twelve she had made the decision to have a normal childhood, and didn't get back into music again until she was in her late twenties. When she met Sharon and Eilleen, Mary was just preparing to release her debut album on RCA, and she had already charted a few country singles in Canada.

Eilleen opened for other recording acts when she was in her early teens—artists who were well-known on the Canadian country circuit, like Gary Buck, Dallas Harms, Anita Perras, Ronnie Prophet and Carol Baker.

Though Eilleen's life revolved around music, she got involved in a wide variety of typical teenage endeavors. She was a good athlete and played basketball and volleyball in high school. She had a great love for gymnastics, and was even on the school team for a few years until she was sidelined by an injury. For a while she held down a job at McDonald's in Timmins.

Family activities were also a part of Eilleen's youth. The Twain family included Eilleen and sisters Carrie-Ann and Jill, and two half brothers, Mark and Darryl, Sharon and Jerry's sons. Eilleen's stepfather, Jerry, was full-blooded Ojibwa, an Aboriginal Canadian group whose traditional territory includes parts of the northeastern U.S. and central Canada. Jerry adopted his three stepdaughters after he married Sharon, and they became members of the Temagami Bear Island First Nation. Their formal Aboriginal status is based on their adoption by Jerry, but Eilleen recalls her mother telling her that her biological father, Clarence Edwards, had Aboriginal ancestry in his family (something that he will not confirm). The Twains often visited Jerry's relatives on the Mattagami reservation, and Eilleen grew up surrounded by a loving and supportive extended Ojibwa family.

Though was raised up in the bustling towns of Timmins and Sudbury, Eilleen frequently spent time outdoors, going camping with her family, learning to snare rabbits with her grandparents and, when she had finished high school, working on a tree-planting crew. It was her grandparents who offered Eilleen some of her most important lessons about the environment and nature. One of Eilleen's most precious childhood memories is of her grandparents taking her out into the backcountry during the winter to show her how to snare rabbits, a skill they had learned as young people growing up in the north. They showed her how to track rabbits by looking for the place that their tracks intersected in the snow.

But music was still a vital part of Eilleen's daily life. By the time she was a teenager, she had begun taking a more active role with her mother in making decisions about her career. Their mutual love of music and dedication to her career may be the two biggest reasons that Eilleen didn't go through the typical rebellious teenage phase. She credits her parents' support and involvement in her music, and the fact that she was so busy performing in bands, for keeping her focused as a teen. In fact, Eilleen was so busy playing music in her final year of high school that she missed her graduation ceremony because of an out-of-town booking.

When Eilleen was still in her teens, she began working during the summers for her father, who had started a tree-planting business near Timmins. She started out as a planter, but quickly moved up to crew foreman. Eilleen supervised a thirteen-man tree-planting crew—all Cree and Ojibwa from Manitoulin Island, Moose Factory, Moosonee and other northern Ontario communities. It was a family business—her grandparents worked in the camp kitchen, her aunt kept books back in Timmins, her mom looked after things in camp and her father ran the forest operations. Some summers Eilleen and her sister Carrie-ann would move a small trailer up to the work site and live in it together.

On weekends in the summer, and during the winter

months when her parents' reforestation company was closed for the season, Eilleen performed with her band in nightclubs around northern and central Ontario. One of the bands she played with was the rock group Longshot. The group, founded by Timmins keyboardist Dave Hartt, became a popular club band. At first they played pop and rock cover songs, but eventually they added original music to their set lists. Hartt recalls how Eilleen, who was only sixteen years old when she joined the band, played the role of consummate musician, assuming a leadership role and talking music late into the night with the boys. The group eventually broke up, and Hartt blames artistic differences— primarily his and Eilleen's—for its demise.

At this point in her career, Eilleen was wavering between rock and country. Though she was known in the Ontario music business as a country singer, she had been playing primarily in rock bands in the Sudbury and Timmins area. Her bands often opened for national recording acts that were touring northern Ontario, such as Trooper and Freddy Fender.

Eilleen's talent, though, had no problem attracting the interest of people who felt that they could secure her a record deal. Before she was even out of high school, she signed up with a manager and went to Nashville to showcase her talent. But the venture didn't result in any interest from record labels, and Eilleen soon slipped back into playing in rock cover bands in Timmins.

After spending ten years cultivating a career as a country singer for their daughter, Sharon and Jerry were suddenly faced with the possibility that Eilleen might turn her back on their favorite music for the more exciting, youth-oriented rock 'n' roll. When Eilleen was in her late teens, Sharon contacted Mary Bailey and asked her for advice.

Sharon and Eilleen had stayed in touch with Mary ever since they'd met her in 1978 at her concert in Sudbury. During the intervening years, Mary had experienced a fair amount of success as a country singer in Canada. Her debut album, *Mystery Lady*, was released by RCA in 1979, and a follow-up *Think of Me*, in 1981. She had a string of singles that did well on the Canadian country charts. Between 1976 and 1988, she released twelve singles, including "Easy Feeling (Loving You)" and "Mystery Lady."

Shortly after Eilleen graduated from high school, Mary bought out her contract from Eilleen's previous manager and took over the role. They began working on a plan to take Eilleen back to Nashville. Despite a great deal of preparation, and some good contacts in the country music capital, Eilleen's second attempt at Nashville, with Mary as her manager, fared no better then her debut trip. When nothing materialized, Mary and Eilleen parted ways amicably, and Eilleen went back to playing in local pop and rock bands.

Eilleen, however, had not forsaken country music entirely. In 1984, when she was nineteen years old, her photo appeared in *Country Music News*, a Canadian publication. The accompanying article referred to Stan Campbell, a Toronto DJ and record producer, and his plans for 1985, which included working with Eilleen on a recording project. The opportunity came when he took her into the studio and recorded a duet featuring Eilleen and country singer Tim Denis called "Heavy on the Sunshine," which appeared on Denis's self-titled debut album later that year.

In 1987, when Eilleen was twenty-one, she realized that

the only way she would ever have any chance at a recording career was to leave Timmins for a bigger music market. She chose Toronto, Canada's version of New York, in an attempt to get closer to music opportunities. While living in Toronto, Eilleen worked as a secretary at a computer school. Soon after she arrived in the big city, tragedy struck her family, and her musical aspirations suddenly seemed insignificant compared with the enormity of her loss. On November 1, 1987, her parents were driving their Chevy Suburban on a rural highway when they were hit by a fully loaded logging truck. They were killed instantly. It was a day that would come to divide Eilleen's life into two parts—the way life was before the accident, and what it became afterward. Because of the unconditional support and love that Sharon and Jerry had given Eilleen her entire life, she was able to find the strength and determination that she needed to take on the responsibilities that were about to irrevocably change her life.

## CHAPTER THREE

# FROM GERSHWIN
## TO MOTOWN

*Friday nights in July were the craziest. The resort was always filled to capacity, making the dinner theater buzz as if it were on the real Las Vegas strip. The weekend cottage season was in full swing, and Deerhurst was one of the places where transplanted Torontonians liked to entertain their guests. Deerhurst's musical dance review—Viva Vegas—was almost always sold out in the summer.*

*Tonight was no different. Parking her pickup truck in the staff parking lot, Eilleen opened the door and was instantly hit by the oppressive midsummer heat. She walked briskly through the dinner theater's staff entrance and headed down the hallway to the dressing room.*

*"Hey, Carl," she called out as she passed a young man dressed in a dinner jacket that was completely covered by silver sequins.*

*"Running a little late, Eilleen?" he kidded her, raising one eyebrow.*

"I had to take my brothers over to a baseball game on the other side of the lake," she called back at him as she disappeared into the dressing room.

She heard the chattering voices of the dancers floating from the room next door. The six dancers who performed in the Las Vegas–style revue that Eilleen sang in shared the small dressing room next to hers, and it was always crammed floor to ceiling with vividly colored ostrich plumes and glittering costumes.

In the singers' dressing room, Eilleen quickly stepped out of her shorts and T-shirt and into a shimmering red, scoop-necked top, black pants and a silver-sequined jacket.

"Cutting it close, aren't you?" a dark-haired woman said to Eilleen, feigning sternness.

"Oh hi, Shania," Eilleen said warmly to the young wardrobe assistant. "Well, the boys slowed me down tonight, but I made it."

As Shania helped with the buttons on the back of her top, Eilleen asked, "You know, Shania, I've always admired your name. What does it mean?"

"It's Ojibwa," Shania answered, "for 'I'm on my way.' "

"That's really beautiful," Eilleen responded quietly. "You know, my dad was Ojibwa."

The two women smiled at each other, then Eilleen let out a small yelp. "Yikes, I'm supposed to be out there right now. Thanks, Shania."

In a blur of sequins and sparkles, Eilleen Twain quietly slipped backstage to wait for her cue to go on.

◆　　　◆　　　◆

In many ways, Eilleen's youth ended the day that her parents died. She became the executor of her parents' estate and guardian of two brothers, ages thirteen and fourteen, and a sister who was eighteen (her older sister, Jill, was raising her own family). Though still grieving, she settled her parents' business affairs and sold their equipment and reforestation company. The musical aspirations and dreams that had taken her to Toronto only a few months earlier were crushed under the weight of adult responsibility and the need to support her family.

The sudden obligations were overwhelming. One of her first instincts after the accident had been to flee from all of the pressures. But she'd stayed and made a commitment to take care of her siblings until they were ready to be on their own.

During this painful crossroads in her life, she felt that she had no choice but to give up music. After her parents' funeral, she left Toronto and moved back to Timmins to take on the role of family matriarch. It was not the first time that she had taken on responsibilities far beyond her years.

At different times, the Twains lived in Timmins, Sudbury and South Porcupine—they moved frequently, hoping to improve their luck or to find work—and they were often the only Aboriginal family on their block. Racism in small towns like Timmins, though not as overt as in larger cities, is still a painful experience for children who are from a different ethnic group. Eilleen zealously and openly protected her brothers from the taunts of other children. But she herself was not immune to the racism—one family wouldn't let her date their son because she was from an Aboriginal family.

There were times in Eilleen's childhood when there wasn't enough food to make lunches for herself and her four siblings. Other times, the family had to scrape together money to pay for the basic necessities. But while Jerry and Sharon didn't always have the material comforts that they might have hoped for, the Twain family was rich in familial ties and support.

These family connections came from the Twain side of the family. There was never any doubt in the extended Twain family that Sharon's three daughters were as important to Jerry as his own two sons were. Once, when he was doing some contract work for the Department of Indian Affairs, he visited the office and proudly showed the staff photographs of his five children. Eilleen grew up with the knowledge that she was Aboriginal, just like her stepfather and half brothers. As she once explained to a reporter years later, when her heritage was being questioned, she may not have been from the same egg as the Twains, but she was from the same nest.

On the nearby Temagami and Mattagami reserves, the Twain family frequently visited Jerry's relatives. Some members of their Ojibwa family still lived off the land, like so many other northerners, both Aboriginal and non-Aboriginal. They trapped and hunted, and as a child Eilleen's diet often included moose, deer and partridge.

In the summers, when the Twains were visiting their relatives on the reserve, they often attended powwows, and Eilleen and her brothers and sisters experienced the stunning display of competitive Aboriginal powwow dancing, drumming and barbecues that are associated with these outdoor Aboriginal celebrations.

When Jerry and Sharon were killed, the extended Twain family—grandparents, aunts, uncles and cousins—were there with support and love for Eilleen and her sisters and brothers. Another person she counted on during that dark, confusing period in her life was John Kim Bell, a young, university-educated Mohawk conductor and classical piano player whose ambition for artistic achievement closely matched Eilleen's. It was John to whom Eilleen turned to talk about her personal loss as well as her musical dreams.

John is a well-known leader in the Aboriginal arts scene in Canada. His twelve-year-old foundation, the National Aboriginal Achievement Foundation (formerly the Canadian Native Arts Foundation), provides training and education grants to Aboriginal Canadian artists, dancers, musicians, singers, writers, filmmakers, choreographers and arts administrators. Although it is now a successful national organization that produces the National Aboriginal Achievement Awards on CBC-TV and that provides hundreds of thousands of dollars in arts training grants every year, the early years of the foundation were a struggle. When he first started out, he diligently set about producing gala fund-raisers to finance the foundation's growth. In the beginning, his biggest fund-raising trump card was his connection to the moneyed worlds of classical and theatrical music in which he had worked—the Toronto Symphony and Broadway, to be precise. His connections provided the collateral that he traded in when he conceived his first big fund-raiser—Bernadette Peters performing with the Toronto Symphony at Roy Thompson Hall in Toronto. The date was February 8,

1987. And one of the opening acts? An up-and-coming singer named Eilleen Twain.

Eilleen performed one of her own songs for the sold-out audience, as well as a duet with Miq'maq classical guitarist Don Ross. While the performance didn't lead to a record deal in Canada, standing onstage in front of a sold-out room in Toronto must have been a strong motivating experience for Shania.

◆　◆　◆

Following her parents' accident, music was the last thing on Eilleen's mind. As the executor of their estate, and the legal guardian of her brothers, Eilleen simply did not have the time to pursue her lifelong dream of a recording deal any longer.

It was Mary Bailey who helped guide Eilleen through her family tragedy and back toward music. From the moment that Mary met Eilleen and Sharon, she'd felt a strong interest in the young girl's career. Now, Mary was eager to take on a half-mother, half-manager relationship with Eilleen. Mary encouraged her to stay in music, and she helped her get an audition at Deerhurst Resort, a posh hotel in Ontario's cottage district.

Though the resort did not have any openings at the time for lead singers, Eilleen's audition impressed the producers so much that they decided to create a part for her, and she was offered a full-time job with the musical theater. Eilleen was wary at first. After all, she had three siblings to support, and she needed stability. The producers at Deerhurst assured her of the security of the job, and Eilleen accepted it. She went back to Timmins and persuaded her brothers and sister to leave their hometown for Huntsville. She moved them south, eventually bought a small house and a pickup truck, and got into the routine of a six-night-a-week performing job at Deerhurst and a seven-day-a-week job as mother-sister to her siblings.

Working at Deerhurst turned out to be a musical education for Shania, and in many ways it fulfilled her childhood dream of attending a performing arts school. The job involved singing different styles of music, from Gershwin to Webber to Motown. She learned to dance, to act and to get out from behind her guitar, which had become a security blanket for her.

It was at Deerhurst that Eilleen adopted the stage name Shania, after the young woman who worked as her costume assistant there. Shania considers the Ojibwa name a tribute to her parents, especially her father, whose parents and grandparents had spoken the language.

In 1990, after three years at Deerhurst, her siblings began moving out one by one. Despite being only twenty-five years old at the time, Eilleen recalls feeling like a middle-aged woman whose kids had all finished school and left home. Without the responsibility of parenting and supporting a family, Shania turned her attention back to pursuing her ultimate goal: a recording contract and a move to Nashville.

Mary Bailey, who had become Eilleen's manager again, contacted Dick Frank, a prominent Nashville entertainment attorney and colleague, to ask if he'd be interested in coming up to Ontario to see a promising young country singer.

Mary wasn't just picking some Nashville insider's name out of a hat when she phoned Dick Frank; she was aware of his excellent reputation in the Nashville music industry. An entertainment attorney for thirty-five years, he was one of the founders of the Country Music Association, a respected and formidable organization in Nashville.

Dick Frank and his wife had always liked Toronto, a city that they would have to go through to get to Huntsville, where Eilleen was working at the Deerhurst Resort. They had also heard about Deerhurst, an elegantly restored hotel in the heart of the Muskogee vacation district.

They arrived from Nashville and checked into their suite at Deerhurst, and that evening went to the dinner theater, where Shania had just finished performing in the musical review.

When the Franks sat down in the nightclub it was near closing time, and they could hear the sound of crockery clanking in the kitchen as the staff cleaned up for the night. In the audience were some of the singers with whom Shania worked in the dinner theater, as well as a few members of her family and some close friends. They all knew how important the showcase was that night. Just the idea of having someone from Nashville in the audience was enough to send tremors of excitement through the small audience.

Dick Frank remembers that it was so quiet in the room when Eilleen came out on the stage that you could have heard a pin drop. Listening to her sing that night, he had the sensation of his hair standing up on the back of his neck. She sang with such an extraordinary amount of musical passion and poise that he knew then and there that she had the potential to be a country superstar.

Less than ten years later, Dick Frank's prediction has come true. And his admiration for Shania has only grown with time—he recently stated that in all his years in the entertainment industry, he's never seen an artist with greater natural talent. He believes Shania is right up there in the company of Lena Horne and Nat "King" Cole.

## CHAPTER FOUR

# A New Kid in Town

*The windshield wipers on the rented tour bus are slapping maniacally back and forth in two-four time, but the spring thunderstorm is simply too intense to keep the windows clear. The storm had been threatening all afternoon, starting out as benign pink-gray clouds on the horizon, then quickly transforming into rolling black clouds as the bus headed straight into them on its route to Houston. The driver was hoping to get his entourage of singers, musicians and technicians to their hotel by midafternoon, but now he was eagerly looking for a roadside diner to pull into so they could wait out the storm. The bus pulled into the first truck stop they came across, the two semis filled with musical and sound equipment following close behind.*

*Shania stood up, yawned and stretched. "I was hoping we'd take a short break."*

*Shania and her label-mates at Mercury Nashville, Toby Keith and John Brannen, had all released debut albums that year, and*

*they were traveling and performing together on a fifteen-city con-*
*cert tour of the South and Southwest.*

*Shania was just about to step out into the torrential downpour*
*when the tour's road manager called to her from inside the bus.*
*"Hey, Shania, I've got your manager on my cell phone. She says*
*it's important."*

*Taking the phone from his hand, she felt a sense of dread mixed*
*with anticipation as she waited to hear what Mary Bailey wanted*
*to tell her. "We've got a director for your next video," Mary*
*said to Shania, "but you've got to call him back within the next*
*half hour."*

*"Call who back?" Shania asked innocently.*

*"Sean Penn," Mary replied, barely concealing her excitement,*
*"wants to direct 'Dance with the One That Brought You.' "*

*Shania let out a yell. "That's amazing," she said a bit too*
*loudly, glancing around at the other musicians on the bus, who*
*were now intently following her every move and word. She found*
*a pen and quickly jotted down Sean Penn's number. As she di-*
*aled it, she thought about how her year had been so far. A debut*
*album, her first single on the* Billboard *charts, a video on Coun-*
*try Music Television, a producer from England who was inter-*
*ested in collaborating on some songs, and possibly her next*
*album. And now this—Sean Penn wanting to direct her video.*
*As she waited for Sean to take her call, she smiled. It doesn't get*
*any better than this, she thought.*

◆   ◆   ◆

The Cascade Conservatory of the Opryland Hotel in
Nashville is a cross between the Amazon and a suburban
mall. Inside the four-acre glass-roofed conservatory, foot-

paths meander through a jungle of palm trees, azaleas and oleanders. Tourists stroll past the carefully groomed indoor tropical paradise, stopping every few feet to admire gold-flecked carp in ponds or to get their pictures taken next to flower arbors. Nearby, quaint shops sell overpriced, vaguely useful designer gifts, and well-heeled guests sip iced teas on restaurant patios.

The Conservatory is the least likely place to find any of the 1,500 country radio executives and programmers who flock to the Opryland Hotel every year to attend the Country Music Seminar. They are too preoccupied by the industry sessions, power breakfasts and musical showcases of some of country music's top acts that take place at the opulent hotel to notice the tropical tourist oasis nearby. This is the one week every year when the people who make music come to win over the people who deliver that music to the masses, through a network of more than 2,500 country radio stations. The CMS is the biggest, and arguably the most important, annual gathering of country radio programmers.

Like all newcomers to Nashville, Shania knew the importance of impressing the decision makers at country radio stations. An artist can never manage to meet the program directors at every country station in Canada and the U.S., but having them on your side can mean the difference between a Top 10 hit and one that gets lost on the CD slush pile the first week it arrives.

At the time of the 1993 CMS, Shania's debut CD, *Shania Twain*, was still weeks away from being officially released, but her single "What Made You Say That" was getting modest airplay on country radio stations.

Shania's debut at this influential conference did not include fireworks or a standing-room-only performance. Like all young artists who pay their dues before making it to the top, Shania spent time sitting at a table in the Mercury Nashville section of the exhibit hall, with stacks of her CD and liner notes spread out neatly in front of her. The publicity department at Mercury Nashville had enlarged the cover of her CD so that the photo of a fur-clad Shania standing in a frozen northern snowdrift was almost as large as the real Shania sitting at the conference trade show table.

It wasn't so much that no one wanted to stop to meet Shania at her table; but the continuous activity only a few feet away from her table was creating a stark contrast. Throughout the day, a constant stream of radio representatives converged on her next-door neighbor's table. Basking in all the adulation was Shania's label-mate at Mercury Nashville, Billy Ray Cyrus. His debut single, "Achy Breaky Heart," had not only spent six weeks as a number one radio hit in 1992, but his debut Mercury album, *Some Gave All*, was on its way to selling close to eight million copies.

By comparison, Shania, who'd signed her record deal with Mercury only a year after Billy had, would sell less than a hundred thousand copies of her debut CD the year it was released. (After Shania scored a hit with her 1995 release, *The Woman in Me*, her debut album would eventually sell half a million copies as a catalog album.) Three singles, and their associated videos, were released from her self-titled debut album, which peaked at number 67 in August 1993 on *Billboard*'s Top Country Albums chart.

At the CMS that year, no one could ever have imagined

that in a few short years, the young dark-haired singer's still unrecorded second CD would become the biggest-selling album by a female artist in the history of country music. Otherwise, a few more of those in Billy's line might have crossed over and spent a little time with Shania.

Dave Kelly, program director at WSIX in Nashville, was one of the few people who stopped at Shania's table that day. He recalls how the bustling crowd at Cyrus's table made hers seem so disarmingly empty. He knew that all new artists have to go through this humiliating period in their career when no one knows who they are, but he felt particularly touched by seeing Shania sitting bravely at her table, a virtual unknown in country music, enthusiastically greeting the few radio executives who stopped by to meet her.

After speaking to Shania for several minutes, he thanked her for her liner notes and moved on. A few years later, when she was eclipsing her label-mates with a number one album on the *Billboard* Top Country Albums chart, Dave Kelly already had information on her from the 1993 conference, and his DJs quickly offered it to an appreciative radio audience. Since then, Shania has appeared several times as a guest on the award-winning WSIX.

Long before Shania became the country music phenomenon of 1995 and 1996, and the darling of country music radio, she was just one of a thousand aspiring singers, songwriters and musicians who try to break into Nashville every year. At bus stations and airports, checking into budget hotels or sleeping on the couches of friends, young men and women converge on Nashville with the dream of landing a record deal or selling a song to a superstar.

Nancy Shapiro, executive director of the Nashville chapter of the National Academy of Recording Arts and Sciences, shakes her head when she talks about how many aspiring musicians flock to Nashville in the hopes of making it big like Garth Brooks or Reba McEntire. It's the great myth of country music that you have to go to Nashville to land a recording contract, she points out. The majority of the country artists who sign with a major record label are discovered far from the bright lights of Nashville, whether it is Austin, Texas or Rome, Georgia. The A & R (Artist and Repertoire) staffs at record labels, whose job it is to discover and sign promising new talent, look for performers who have already proven they can attract a loyal following in their own region, or acts who have seen some success with an independently released album. Some of these successful regional artists are brought up to the major leagues, and with the right team of music professionals and a little luck, they establish the recording careers that they have aspired to since childhood.

Shania Twain, Shapiro says, made it in Nashville the right way. Shania worked hard at her music in her own region, wrote original songs and developed her musical style before taking a crack at Nashville. Shania had first-hand knowledge of how not to pursue a recording deal in Nashville—she had tried twice before with two different managers when she was in her late teens, and she had gone back home empty-handed each time. The key to Shania's success the third time was Nashville attorney Dick Frank.

The showcase at Deerhurst had totally impressed Frank. He agreed to work with Mary Bailey to find Shania a recording contract in Nashville. Soon after the showcase,

Shania left Deerhurst Resort, returned to Timmins and began perfecting the songs that would become her demo tape
for Nashville. She took a job at the complaints desk at Sears
department store, but she had no doubt in her mind that
the job would be temporary.

Within weeks, Dick Frank called Mary with the news
that he had arranged for Norro Wilson, a first-rate producer, to record Shania's demo tape in Nashville. Mary put
up the money for the two of them to travel to Nashville
and for the cost of musicians and studio time to record the
demo. Shania and Norro worked together to find the right
songs to highlight her evocative voice and versatile style.
Meanwhile, Dick Frank set about looking after some legal
concerns for Shania.

Dick, Mary and Norro knew that Shania had superstar
potential, and they wanted to handpick her label rather
than approach every major country label and wait for an
offer they would be satisfied with.

After discussing the pros and cons of several labels, they
chose Mercury Nashville as the one that could offer her the
most. The label is owned by PolyGram, an international
corporation with offices and sales and promotion staff in
the U.S., Canada, Europe, Australia and other countries, an
important feature for an artist with international potential,
as they felt Shania had. Mercury wasn't saturated with
stars with overblown egos that required inordinate
amounts of stroking by staff, as some other labels were.
They felt that she would get the kind of attention from the
executives and staff at Mercury Nashville that was so critical in breaking a promising new artist.

Dick Frank handed Shania's demo tape to Buddy Cannon, who was head of A & R at Mercury Nashville at the time. Cannon championed Shania at his label and brought her tape to the company's president, Harold Shedd. Shedd called Frank after he heard Shania's tape and said he was interested in talking terms. Amazingly, it was the first and only label that ever had the opportunity to sign her, and Mercury eagerly entered into a multirecord deal with the Canadian beauty. It was Harold Shedd who is credited with signing Shania to Mercury Nashville, however, Luke Lewis had been appointed president when her debut CD was released in 1993.

Mercury Nashville is one of dozens of country music companies that have offices in an area on the south side of Nashville known as Music Row.

The office buildings that are clustered along Music Row and Music Circle East, West, South and North are an eclectic mixture of steel and glass low-rise office buildings and turn-of-the-century historic houses. The Nashville music district, with its mix of recording studios, music publishing companies, music publications, radio stations, record labels and management companies is like a self-contained music empire.

At its northern border, the Country Music Hall of Fame is a hornet's nest of activity, with hundreds of thousands of country music fans a year making the pilgrimage to the museum, which attempts, through colorful, interactive exhibits, to explain the seventy-five-year history of country music.

Just a few blocks away, fiercely protective receptionists guard the offices of music industry executives like sentries guarding the crown jewels. Musicians and songwriters spend their entire careers trying to get into the offices of the decision makers in Nashville, but some get no closer than the ticket sellers at the Country Music Hall of Fame.

When Twain arrived in Nashville in the early 1990s, she was both a Canadian and outside the "country music circle." The fertile breeding ground of country music artists has traditionally been limited to a rather broad path across the American South, from Georgia to Texas and from the Gulf States to as far north as Kentucky. Though every now and then a musician from California or Ohio slips in through the cracks, these are the exceptions rather than the rule. What few American country fans are aware of is that the majority of Canada, from the prairie provinces to Ontario to the Atlantic region, has just as rich a country music tradition as the American South and Southwest. Despite Shania's northern Canadian roots, she had been through all the rites of passage that many of her southern colleagues can boast—a hardworking, blue-collar upbringing, years of poverty and a family that celebrated country music with unbridled enthusiasm.

Shania Twain's self-titled debut album was released in April 1993. All but one of the songs on the album were written by professional Nashville songwriters. Shania, whose own songwriting skills apparently did not satisfy her producers, Norro Wilson and Harold Shedd, contributed only one tune, "God Ain't Gonna Getcha for That."

In reality, some of her own songs on her second release, *The Woman in Me,* existed in one form or another when she was recording her first album. They were destined to be put on hold until she could find a producer who could take her musical efforts and give each song a full, rich life of its own.

But in many ways, there really wasn't any alternative to the way that her first album evolved. Shania obviously had some wonderful, but underdeveloped, songs for her producers to consider. When they decided to pass on them, Shania did what most first-time recording artists would have done: respected the opinion of her seasoned producers. She was, after all, new in Nashville, and was there to absorb as much knowledge as she could during her first recording project. Over time, she would be able to build up some credibility and start establishing some of her own criteria for her albums. That time had not yet arrived in 1993.

Wilson and Shedd chose to shop for the "right songs" for Shania's debut album rather than try to develop Shania's existing material. This is a standard approach to recording an artist who doesn't write his or her own songs or who doesn't have enough strong material to create a "sound" for an album.

Shania's ability at handling a wide variety of styles comes through in her debut CD, but there is a lack of emotional depth in the material that was chosen for her. Although Shania's lack of connection to the people and stories that inhabit the songs in her first recording may have kept it from being an entirely convincing effort, it was nonetheless a respectable debut. Three singles were released off her debut album: "What Made You Say That," which peaked at number 55 on May 22, 1993; "Dance with the One That Brought You," which climbed to the same spot on the *Billboard* Hot Country Singles chart on August 21, 1993; and "You Lay a Whole Lot of Love on Me," which failed to make it to the charts.

Despite only modest sales of her first release, the CD did garner her a Country Music Television Europe Rising Star award, and earned her the number seven spot on *Billboard* magazine's 1993 list of promising new artists.

Every year, when a new crop of country artists is launched by record labels, there's always the possibility that the media or radio stations simply won't take notice. Mercury Nashville had three promising young country acts in 1993, and it wanted to get as much exposure for them as possible. Rather than follow the traditional route of sending each act out on the concert circuit to open for an established recording group or solo artist, Mercury sent the three new acts out on tour together.

Dubbed the "Triple Play" tour, it took Shania and her label-mates Toby Keith and John Brannen on a fifteen-city tour through the southern and southwestern United States. Though there were reported artistic differences among the three of them, the tour gave Shania the opportunity to perform live in a concert setting, something that she would not do again until May 1998, after the release in November 1997 of her third album, *Come on Over*.

It was while she was on the road with Toby and John that manager Mary Bailey called her with the exciting news that Sean Penn, Hollywood bad boy and aspiring filmmaker, wanted to direct her in a video for the single "Dance with the One That Brought You." Shania, who was truly at the starting block of her career at the time, was thrilled by the interest from Penn, and the resulting collaboration has the most traditional country feel of all her videos.

Penn was not the only well-known entertainment figure

who found Shania intriguing. Across the Atlantic Ocean, Robert John "Mutt" Lange, one of rock music's most respected and successful producers, saw Shania's video of "What Made You Say That," on CMT Europe and was sufficiently impressed to call her label in Nashville and ask for her manager's number. His interest in Shania, a virtually unknown country artist at the time, is hard to comprehend at first glance. Mutt, after all, is a veteran of the hard rock and pop music scene, having produced albums and written songs for AC/DC, the Cars, Michael Bolton, Def Leppard, Bryan Adams and Foreigner. Shania Twain, a quasi-traditional country singer from Timmins, Ontario, just didn't seem to fit into this impressive roster of major arena acts.

Mutt, it turns out, is a closet country fan; Shania claims that country music is his greatest love. Whether it was a professional or personal fixation he had on Shania, he was captivated enough to try to get in touch with her.

When Mutt got through to Mary, she assumed that he was a fan, and she sent him an autographed photo of Shania. Neither she nor Shania had ever heard of him, which is not too surprising, since their world revolved around country, not glam rock.

Perhaps mildly amused, Mutt remained persistent, until he finally got through to Shania on the phone. On their first transatlantic conversation, Mutt encouraged Shania to sing a few of her songs to him. Shania's first CD had featured only one of her songs, but she had persuaded Mercury to give her the chance to record some more of her original music for her second CD. One of the first things that Mutt wanted to know was whether she wrote her own material. She was flattered by his interest in her songwriting and she sang him "Home Ain't Where His Heart Is (Anymore)" over the phone. Mutt immediately recognized a promising, if somewhat underdeveloped, songwriter. Over the next several weeks, the two discussed, by telephone, songs and musical ideas. Shania's musical self-esteem soared, knowing that she was connecting on a profoundly intimate musical level with one of the industry's most prolific and successful songwriters and producers.

The first meeting between Shania and Mutt took place in Nashville at Fan Fair in June 1993. Mutt had been working on an album with Canadian singer Bryan Adams (the critically acclaimed *18 'Til I Die* CD that was released in 1994) in Jamaica, and he and Bryan decided to fly to Nashville for the country music event of the year. He approached her fan booth, and when he introduced himself, Shania, who claims not to be a "huggy person," gave him a big hug. After three months of getting to know each other on the phone, they were finally meeting face-to-face.

Fan Fair '93 was another first for Shania. She was one of the featured performers at Mercury Nashville's showcase, along with her label-mates John Brannen, Toby Keith and Billy Ray Cyrus.

Soon after first meeting Shania at Fan Fair that year, Mutt invited her to France, where he was working on the production of Bryan's CD. It was in France that their professional relationship progressed to a romantic one, and it was there that he proposed to her. On December 28, 1993, only six months after meeting in person, Shania and Mutt Lange were married at Deerhurst Resort.

It would be the beginning of more than a life together for Shania and Mutt—the stage was set for the two to become one of the most successful songwriting teams in the history of country music.

## CHAPTER FIVE

# LANGE AND TWAIN: A WINNING TEAM

*Even before she sees their faces, the cashier at the grocery store in the small upstate New York town knows them from the odd array of food in their shopping cart—organic zucchini, basmati rice, arugula lettuce, Chinese leeks, tofu and soy milk. When she looks up from her cash register to say good morning, the woman always offers her a warm, casual greeting and a smile that could only come from someone raised in a small town. The man is usually on the quiet side, but when he does speak, to ask the woman if she remembered to buy a certain item, his accent hints of a proper British upbringing.*

*In the two or three years that the couple have been shopping there, the cashier has always wondered how such an unlikely twosome ever got together. Her guess is that the woman is at least fifteen years younger than her husband. Physically, they seem an improbable match. The woman is petite and stunningly beautiful, with wide-set chocolate eyes, high cheekbones and lustrous brown hair. Her husband is almost a foot taller, with a stocky build, ruddy complexion and long blond hair that gives him the air of an aging rock star.*

*A couple of times she's heard the woman humming a song quietly to herself while waiting in the checkout line with her cart. And once, when she was ringing up her order, the woman seemed preoccupied, not in her usual conversational mood. She could hear her quietly repeating a line of a song over and over, as if she was afraid that if she stopped, the melody would be erased from her memory.*

*The cashier smiled to herself that day, knowing that she'd probably just witnessed a little bit of country music history. And to this day, she's convinced that one of the songs from the woman's CD bears an uncanny resemblance to the melody that she heard her singing quietly to herself as she placed her broccoli and miso soup on the conveyor belt.*

◆　◆　◆

There's a rumor that Shania Twain is married. The brilliant 2.5-carat diamond on her ring finger is one piece of circumstantial evidence. The inordinate number of times the name of her purported spouse, Robert John "Mutt" Lange, appears on the credits of her second and third CD—producer, cosongwriter, background singer, guitarist—certainly implies an ongoing professional affiliation. And the media has reported on their alleged alliance on numerous occasions, including a private wedding at Deerhurst Resort on December 28, 1993. There are just very few actual sightings of the two of them together.

Despite the fact that Mutt is one of the music industry's

most reclusive characters, he has had a profound effect on the professional and personal life of Shania Twain. He is, without question, the single most influential man in her life other than her stepfather, Jerry.

On the most basic levels, however, Shania and Mutt are a study in contrasts. He shuns the spotlight, despite being a world-class producer and songwriter; she is a media fly trap, having been interviewed on almost every news, entertainment and talk show on cable and network television, as well as by hundreds of newspapers and magazines in Canada and the U.S. Mutt's idea of a public act is asking the gas station attendant to check the oil in his car; Shania's is jumping up and down on a stage singing "Any Man of Mine" a cappella in front of 20,000 screaming fans at a midwestern shopping mall.

The contrasts continue. He is tall (six foot), blond, with British citizenship after immigrating from South Africa; she is petite (five foot four), brunette, a resident alien in America after immigrating from Canada. He drives a European sports car; she favors four-wheel drives. He loathes public gatherings, and never appears at his own or his wife's awards ceremonies; Shania's primary social life revolves around the Los Angeles–Nashville–New York music awards show circuit every year.

With only one media interview known to exist (in an obscure British recording industry magazine in the 1980s), there is virtually no published biographical material on Mutt Lange. Writing a profile of Robert John "Mutt" Lange is like doing a blind taste test of a soft drink. You know it's a cola you're drinking, but without getting to see the label, you only have a limited sense of the product. Shania, however, is one of Mutt's biggest fans, and affectionately shares anecdotes about him whenever she is being interviewed.

The story of how Shania and Mutt met has been retold in the media so many times that it has taken on the characteristics of urban folklore. The oft-told story rarely alters from the basic facts: Mutt made an attempt to contact Shania after seeing her video on CMT Europe, and was brushed off by Mary Bailey with an autographed photograph of Shania. When he finally got through to her, and they started their long-distance phone relationship, Shania wasn't even aware of his international reputation as a famous producer. When she found out, she pretended she had always known. They got to know each other honestly, Shania claims, and it was not his success or money that charmed her. It turned out that almost every album he ever produced was on her favorite-record list.

Mutt and Shania's initial three-hour gabfests between Europe and the States were the foundation of the personal and musical relationship that was to evolve. Until that point, Shania had never been treated with so much respect for her songwriting abilities. After the deflating experience of having her songs rejected by the producers of her first album, Mutt's fascination with them must have been a redeeming, and esteem-building, experience for Shania.

The fact is, Shania had been writing and performing her own songs for close to twenty years. When she met Mutt on the phone, she felt an immediate connection because he was talking her language. During their very first conversation, he asked her to sing one of the songs she'd been working on. She sang him "Home Ain't Where His Heart Is (Anymore)," strumming the guitar, with the phone propped up on a pillow. In return, he played a song he'd been working on, Michael Bolton's "Said I Loved You But I Lied."

When Shania sang that first song for Mutt, her clear alto voice traveling across thousands of miles of optic fibers, Mutt's creative heart must have skipped a beat. He had initially noticed Shania's stunning beauty and singing talent when he saw her video of "What Made You Say That" on CMT Europe. But now that they were sharing her works-in-progress, Mutt discovered that he was dealing with a multitalented musician and songwriter. His lifelong love of country music, and his reputation for crossing musical genres many times in his career as a producer, made it perfectly reasonable for him to pursue Shania on a professional level.

Over the next three months, via the telephone, they began to explore each other's creative side. By the time they met in June 1993, they had built up a level of trust and respect for each other that would be the foundation for their future personal and professional relationships.

Mercury Nashville had already indicated to Shania that it would let her record some of her own music on the follow-up to her debut album. The timing was perfect for Mutt and Shania to approach the label with their plan to have Mutt produce the album. Luke Lewis, the label's president, knew it was a musical opportunity of a lifetime for both Shania and Mercury. Although Mutt was not a household name in country music, his remarkable success as a producer of rock and pop music acts had made him a music industry legend. Together, Mutt and Shania had enough credibility to be turned loose in the studio, and be virtually guaranteed a hit album.

Perhaps even more stunning than his offer to produce was Mutt's commitment to personally finance an enhanced version of the record; in other words, he would become an investor, along with Mercury Nashville, in Shania's career. The diamond engagement ring may have been a classic symbol of Mutt's love for Shania, but his offer to bankroll her future album project went beyond love and honor. And he was undoubtedly getting something valuable out of the proposition as well. By producing Shania, he was able to explore a musical genre that he had always loved—country music. Shania's dowry, in a way, was the musical opportunity that Mutt had always coveted. It truly was a partnership made in music heaven.

It took a year and a half and more than half a million dollars to complete *The Woman in Me*. The cost stunned Nashville, where most album budgets come in at a tenth of that amount.

The album, released in January 1995, featured twelve songs, ten cowritten by Mutt and Shania and a solo effort by each. Shania had been working on at least ten of the songs before she met Mutt. The reaction from Nashville insiders, country radio programmers and media record reviewers was that Mutt had contributed the rock and pop elements of *The Woman in Me*, and Shania the country elements. Shania disputes this theory; explaining that Mutt's real love is country music and that the country production qualities on the album, including the dominant steel guitar and fiddle influences, were his. Shania herself has a broad range of musical interests, from country to rock to pop to soul, and she was eager to branch out into different directions.

Mutt's imprint on the album, besides the obvious brilliant production values, was that he took Shania's attitude and creativity and made the songs uniquely hers—rather than taking songs and trying to mold Shania to them, as was the case in her first release. His ability to do this could well have had its origins in their private world. Who else but Mutt could have known the depth of Shania's musical personality; after all, he was seeing it every day at home.

In fact, Shania often describes this scene as being typical of the way they write music together: Mutt will be in the living room watching a hockey game, his guitar in his hands (Shania claims that Mutt always has a guitar with him). She'll be in the kitchen cooking. She'll sing a line of a song, and he'll put some music to it. Then she'll call out and ask him to try it in another key. And on and on. The Langes, Shania jokingly says, are a two-guitar household.

Another role that Mutt played on their first album together was getting Shania to listen to her songs from new angles and then encouraging her to infuse her own identity into them. "Any Man of Mine," for instance, was originally called "That Man of Mine," before the two revamped it from an adoring, male-focused song to an assertive declaration of a woman's expectations in a relationship. The song is considered her breakthrough single on the album, and it was her first number one hit.

Shania and Mutt have been collaborating on her music for five years and two albums now, and they've had the time to uncover and analyze each other's musical strengths and weaknesses. Shania, however, does not hold the record for number of albums recorded with Mutt at the board. That honor is held by AC/DC, with four.

His career as a recording technician was launched in England in the 1970s, working on albums by Graham Parker and XTC. Mutt wrote a number of landmark 1980s rock songs, including "Photograph" for Def Leppard, "Loving Every Minute of It" for Loverboy and "Do You Believe in Love" for Huey Lewis and the News. In the 1990s, he became a major collaborator on pop-rock songs, perhaps having evolved beyond the arena head-banger rock of AC/DC and Def Leppard.

He has been a musical mentor, genius and savior to some of the most successful acts of the 1980s and 1990s—AC/DC, Def Leppard, Foreigner, the Cars, Bryan Adams, Michael Bolton, Journey and Billy Ocean. Collectively, the albums that he has produced have sold more than 110 million copies. His songs and albums have been nominated for Academy Awards, Junos and Grammys, and a number of them have been used on the sound tracks of Hollywood movies, including Shania's "No One Needs to Know" (*Twister*), Bryan Adams's "Have You Ever Really Loved a Woman?" (*Don Juan DeMarco*), and "Everything I Do I Do for You" (*Robin Hood: Prince of Thieves*).

In 1994, Mutt was honored as the ASCAP Songwriter of the Year, having cowritten three of the most performed songs: Bryan Adams's "All for Love" and "Please Forgive

Me," and Michael Bolton's "Said I Loved You But I Lied." In 1995, three of the most played songs of the year were written by Mutt and Shania: "Any Man of Mine," "Whose Bed Have Your Boots Been Under?" and "The Woman in Me."

Mutt's reputation as a phenomenal producer and songwriter keeps him in high demand, regardless of artists' musical leanings. According to Michael Bolton, who has recorded two albums with Mutt, nothing is too good for the "Mutt Man," even if that means Michael's perception of time goes out the window. He admiringly calls Mutt the "Steven Spielberg of music." He also calls him a pit bull in the studio, and says that working with Mutt is the hardest work he does.

Collaborating with Mutt is different for each artist—Bryan Adams calls him a "great songwriting partner," and says that the ideas come quickly when they're working together.

Shania's collaboration with her husband has resulted in bringing her songwriting standards to a higher level. On a personal level, Shania asserts that Mutt has put her in touch with her sensitive side, that his strength has given her permission to be vulnerable and not always the one making the decisions and having to take the biggest share of responsibility, character traits that can be traced back to her youth.

Living together on a remote 3,000-acre estate in the Adirondack wilderness in upstate New York leaves a lot of time for a couple to discover each other. Shania has stated that Mutt plays a lot of important roles in her life—counselor, lover, friend, producer. If Mutt was ever to reveal his private feelings about his wife to a writer (not likely to happen in the foreseeable future), he might describe Shania as the one person in his life who has made all his songs come true.

CHAPTER SIX

# THE POWER OF MUSIC

*There's an eerie calm that descends on Manhattan when the last waning moments of night cross over into the first hint of a new morning. The manic activity of the night before has ground to a temporary halt—the restaurants and nightclubs and theaters are black, the late-night street action has ebbed for the moment, the endless flow of cabs taking people home after a night out has slowed to a few random cars, the persistent wailing of ambulances and police cars has been silenced.*

*The black sedan carrying Shania Twain through the near-empty predawn streets of Manhattan pulls up to a side entrance at ABC Studios, where guests of* Live! . . . With Regis & Kathie Lee *arrive five days a week for early morning tapings.*

*Shania, sans makeup, her hair tied up in a loose ponytail, steps out of the car. Before her eyes manage to adjust their focus from the dark interior of the car to the amber light of the street, a camera flashes in front of her. Then another. A small group of people—a dozen or so, mostly twenty- and thirty-something women and a couple of younger men—greet Shania enthusiastically as she steps onto the sidewalk. One woman passes Shania a purple spiral-bound notebook. "Would you mind signing this for me?" she asks good-naturedly. Shania smiles back, suddenly realizing that this is not a group of disgruntled union members on a picket line—these are her fans!*

*She signs a few autographs, waves a friendly good-bye and is shuffled into the building by a security guard and a staff member from* Live! . . . With Regis & Kathie Lee.

*In the elevator, Shania turns to Allison and David, the two musicians who will perform with her that morning on an acoustic version of "Any Man of Mine."*

*"Jeez, were those people waiting for me?" she asks in disbelief. It's only been a few weeks since* The Woman in Me *reached the number one spot on the* Billboard's *Top Country Albums chart, and only her second television (other than on video) appearance, after Jay Leno's show a few weeks earlier. "I mean, did they actually wake up early and come down here just to get an autograph?"*

*"You've never been stampeded by fans before?" the ABC staffer asks her in disbelief. "Where have they been hiding you?"*

*Shania laughs nervously. "Well, actually, I really didn't expect to be recognized in New York."*

*"Just give it a little time," the staffer says with a smile, "and you won't be able to walk down a single street in this country without being recognized."*

*The elevator door opens and Shania and her entourage step into the lobby of Studio C at ABC Studios. Shania is shuffled into the green room to await her makeup and hair call. In a matter of hours, millions of daytime television viewers will get their first "live" look at country's new number one superstar.*

◆   ◆   ◆

Shania is somewhat of an anomaly in Nashville. Though she spent much of her early career working toward the goal of making it from Timmins to Nashville, her Canadian roots and lack of southern influences made her an outsider when she arrived there in the early 1990s. And despite her huge success and its reflective glow upon Nashville, the industry has never embraced Shania with unconditional acceptance. The biggest reason is that Shania does not fit the definition of a pure "country artist." It is an accusation that dogged Patsy Cline, another country-pop crossover phenomenon, throughout her career. Upon close inspection, however, Shania may be closer to Nashville's country roots than she's given credit for in that city.

If you strip down the music on *The Woman in Me* you'll find the qualities most revered among country music purists: the jaunty two-step beat of "Any Man of Mine," the classic country swing of "Whose Bed Have Your Boots Been Under?" the harmonica-laden "(If You're Not in It for Love) I'm Outta Here!" and the fiddle-driven "If It Don't Take Two." Then there's the ever-present pedal steel guitar accenting virtually every song on the CD, the Floyd Cramer–influenced piano and the country-laced harmonies.

Shania's songs unquestionably pay homage to the roots of country, and at their leanest would appeal to the most loyal of country fans. But Shania and Mutt chose not to limit the songs on *The Woman in Me* to rigid parameters defined by the Nashville traditionalists. Classic country may be at the core of Shania's music, but there are liberal helpings of Cajun, rock, pop and gospel. The mix, considered renegade by some, propelled *The Woman in Me* straight into the open arms of millions of people who had never before visited the country section of a record store.

The astounding performance of this album—from its meteoric rise and hold on *Billboard*'s Top Country Albums chart (twenty-nine weeks at number one) to its powerful impact on the country music industry in 1995 and 1996— made *The Woman in Me* one of the most analyzed music phenomena of the decade. Shania was the subject of adulation as well as intense criticism by those inside and outside the country music industry. Countless debates took place publicly and privately in Nashville—at radio programming conferences, in the music press and between record company insiders over drinks: Was Shania's talent real? Was she a product of studio wizardry that would never hold up to live performances? Were her visually lush and provocative videos simply a brilliant marketing plan to attract the libidos of men? The only relevant responses came from the real critics—the thirteen million fans who bought her CD after its January 1995 release. In fact, fourteen months later, Shania became the biggest-selling country female artist of all time, outselling Patsy Cline's posthumously released album of greatest hits. The brouhaha over authenticity, it turned out, was of little consequence.

Shania's success can be traced to four sources: the voice, the songs, the producer and the visuals (not necessarily in that order).

The most significant instrument on Shania's second, breakthrough album, *The Woman in Me,* is her voice. Her twangless vocals capture the emotional requirement of every song. Poignant, frivolous, melancholy or jaunty, Shania creates a distinct atmosphere for each song.

The songs, characterized by eloquent and clever lyrics, are the perfect vehicle for a voice that emotes such an amazing range of character. Shania and Mutt share co-writing credit on ten songs, and each claim a solo effort. The album includes five ballads, six uptempo songs and one a cappella gospelesque tune. Though the songs are diverse, there are some clusters of thematic strands running through the album: the classic country losing-at-love ballads ("Home Ain't Where His Heart Is," "Is There Life After Love?" "Raining on Our Love" and "Leaving Is the Only Way Out"); the exquisite this-is-the-real-thing ballad ("The Woman in Me"); the spirited girls-rule songs ("Any Man of Mine," and "(If You're Not in It for Love) I'm Outta Here" and "Whose Bed Have Your Boots Been Under?"; the perky love-rules songs ("If It Don't Take Two," "You Win My Love" and "No One Needs to Know"); and the poignant bare-the-soul song ("God Bless the Child").

The element that makes *The Woman in Me* stand out from among the hundreds of other country albums released in 1995 is its exemplary production quality. Though it's not surprising that her renowned rock producer husband would introduce pop and rock influences into Shania's music—wailing electric guitar licks and tight beats—the songs never forget the country place that they come from. The production, however, is not limited to the lean sound so typical of country music albums. *The Woman in Me* is multilayered, the result of exceptional musical direction and the influence of some of Nashville's best studio musicians.

The visual messages related to *The Woman in Me* have proven to be as much a conversation point as the musical aspects of the album. The earliest images of Shania were completely dominated by the lens of the late photographer and video director John Derek. When Mary Bailey first approached John to mastermind the visual identity of the album, he balked. With his wife Bo's encouragement, he committed to the project. John and Bo (who received a "Photography Assistant" credit on the album) were largely responsible for the "look" that etched Shania forever into the minds of music consumers. John shot the cover photos for the album, plus a promotional calendar featuring Shania that was mailed to retailers and radio stations. The couple also produced and directed Shania's first two videos, "Whose Bed Have Your Boots Been Under?" and "Any Man of Mine." Shania, who already possesses natural beauty, was suddenly elevated to a sultry goddess in front of John's camera.

Another powerful symbol of Shania's visual identity became the most widely discussed body part in country music—her belly button. It appeared subtly at first, then as her own unique trademark, like Cindy Crawford's beauty mark. When Susan Ormiston, a reporter for CTV's newsmagazine *W-5*, interviewed Shania, she asked her if she owned a shirt that went to her waist. "Well, here you go," Shania answered as she glanced down at her shirt, intending to prove Susan wrong. "Well, I guess this one doesn't." With all the emphasis on Shania's midriff, it isn't a surprise that Mercury Nashville placed an ad promoting her album in *Sports Illustrated*'s 1995 college basketball preview issue.

It was the videos, however, that caused the biggest flap.

There's always been a cardinal rule in country music—good girl singers flaunt their hair, not their bodies. Shania quickly broke that archaic rule. Though never overtly sexual, her videos were nonetheless sexy. But the image that at first caused great concern at Mercury Nashville, whose marketing staff feared that Shania would alienate the important female consumer, turned out to be a promoter's dream—a photogenic poster girl who managed to thrill the men and inspire the women with great songs. Not only did Shania score a major identity coup with her video images, she launched an international fashion craze for short tops during the summers of 1995 and 1996.

Initially, the now classic video of Shania teasingly dancing around a stoic bunch of blue-collar guys at a diner for the song "Whose Bed Have Your Boots Been Under?" was almost rejected by CMT. The female-heavy committee that reviews and recommends videos for rotation at the Nashville-based station called the video redundant and too sexy. Even when the single was climbing up the radio charts and Mercury Nashville president Luke Lewis was making weekly calls to the station to ask it to consider giving the video more airplay, CMT relegated it to light rotation. It was Shania's second single, "Any Man of Mine," that became her breakthrough song. By then, viewer requests were so overwhelming for the clip that CMT began to get behind Shania. TNN picked up "Any Man of Mine," and the rest is history. By mid-July, Shania had the number one video on both stations.

There is a fifth, virtually overlooked, reason for her remarkable achievements during 1995 and 1996: her live performances with her band. While she was winning more than her weight in Lucite, teak and brass music awards (the 1995 American Music Awards' Favorite New Country Artist; the 1996 Grammy for Best Country Album; 1996 Country Music Television/Europe awards for Video of the Year—"Any Man of Mine"—and Female Artist of the Year; 1996 Academy of Country Music awards for Top New Female Vocalist and Album of the Year; three 1996 Juno awards; 1996 Canadian Country Music Association awards for Female Vocalist, Video of the Year and Fans Choice Entertainer of the Year; a World Music Award for Best-Selling Female Country Artist; and numerous others), a loyal and talented core group of musicians were jetting around with her in the United States, Great Britain and Canada. The band performed with her on dozens of high-profile television talk shows, and at industry showcases, award ceremonies and Nashville's Fan Fair in 1995 and 1996. Though not a replacement for a full-fledged stadium tour, these mini-performances unquestionably proved her credibility as a musician.

Between her "Triple Play" tour of 1993 and the launch of *The Woman in Me* in 1995, Shania's musical appearances were limited to the annual Mercury showcase each June at Fan Fair in Nashville. Backed by a semiregular group of musicians that included some of her "Triple Play" tour veterans and Nashville session musicians, Shania was able to satisfy the musical requirements of these occasional gigs. Within weeks of releasing her second CD, though, it became apparent to Shania and Mutt that she needed a more permanent band.

The Nashville musicians were initially considered for the job of Shania's backup band. But this idea quickly lost out to logistics. For one thing, Shania and Mutt lived in upstate New York, on a 3,000-acre estate complete with recording studio and guest house. Rehearsing and working with a band 1,500 miles from home in Tennessee would be a huge time and financial burden.

The plan to go out on tour with *The Woman in Me* was part of the impetus for recruiting a northern New York–based band. Another motivation for putting a band together was the speculation that Shania might have to perform on television at some point. Shania didn't want to perform to recorded tracks on TV. Both she and Mutt wanted her music to benefit from the immediacy and power that can only be achieved with a live, working band.

The initial goal was to find an existing, competent, regional Country Rock act and to hire them as Shania's band. The group would ideally be close enough to Mutt and Shania's Lake Placid area home to rehearse regularly. If a ready-made band could not be found, then they would configure one from regional musicians.

In early April 1995, a small classified ad appeared in an Albany, New York–based music and arts magazine called *Metroland:* "Musicians wanted for touring for a well established country artist. All styles of playing are acceptable. Please call Sheri Thorn at—"

The first musician to answer the ad was a lead guitarist from Albany named David Malachowski. A graduate of Berklee College of Music in Boston, David was equally comfortable in a country or rock environment, having toured with recording artists Janie Fricke, John Michael Montgomery and Greg Austin as well as with a number of regional rock acts. In fact, his long hair and penchant for wearing black gave him more the air of a rock 'n' roller than a Nashville player.

David called the number listed in the ad and Sheri Thorn answered the phone. She told him that he was the first person to respond (not surprising, since David, who writes album and concert reviews for *Metroland*, had picked up the latest issue hot off the presses that day). The artist who was looking for a band, Sheri explained, was named Shania Twain and she had released her second album on the Mercury Nashville label only a few months earlier. She had written all the material, and was looking for a regional band to back her up for guest appearances.

David was a bit skeptical. After all, what was a country artist with a record deal doing looking for a band in upstate New York? David put a call in to a musician he knew in Nashville, Tony King (a songwriter who currently plays with Brooks and Dunn). Tony informed David that a friend, musician-songwriter Randy Thomas, had done shows with Shania, and that she was "very cool." Then he dropped the bomb: Shania's husband and producer was Mutt Lange. David knew that he had just connected with a world-class project.

Shania was still a relatively unknown country artist at the time. Her first single off *The Woman in Me*, "Whose Bed Have Your Boots Been Under?" was not destined to hit the ceiling at number 11 on *Billboard*'s Hot Country Singles chart until late April, and the second single, "Any Man of Mine," was still several weeks away from release. David was intrigued enough, though, to send his resume to Sheri at Twain Zone by overnight express.

A few days later, David received a message from Sheri

on his answering machine: "Got your resume; looks great. You aren't by any chance playing in the area this weekend? If you are, leave me directions on my machine."

David met Shania and Mutt for the first time a few days later. He was playing a gig in a small nightclub near Burlington, Vermont, and during the last set of the evening, a tall, long-haired blond man walked into the club with a petite, dark-haired woman. They were both casually dressed, and she wore her hair up in a ponytail. They took seats by a railing, and unlike most of the others in the audience, did not order drinks or get up on the dance floor. After a song or two, the woman looked toward David, smiled and waved. It was Mutt and Shania.

After about an hour of listening intently, Mutt walked over to the side of the stage where David was playing and motioned that he had something to say. As David continued to play, Mutt discreetly said, "I've seen all I need to see. You're great. I'll call you." Then he and Shania left the club.

Less than a week later, David received a message on his machine. A voice with a British accent said, "Hello, David. This is Mutt Lange calling. I'd like to talk to you about putting a band together."

David had already given a lot of thought to the composition of the "perfect" band for Shania. Having lived and played in numerous bands in upstate New York for ten years, and having written about the music scene for *Metroland* for a few years, he knew almost every musician within 150 miles who had any recording or national touring experience. Only a few hours away from New York, David had access to some of the greatest musicians in the country, both from Manhattan as well as other cities scattered across the region. David's dream band included Gary Burke (formerly with Bob Dylan and Joe Jackson) on drums, Graham Maby (Joe Jackson, Freddy Johnston) on bass, Shane Fontayne (Lone Justice, Peter Gabriel, Bruce Springsteen) on guitar, and Allison Cornell (Joe Jackson, Pat Benatar) on fiddle and keyboards. And, of course, David Malachowski (Janie Fricke, John Michael Montgomery) on lead guitar.

The next time David talked to Mutt, he mentioned the names of the musicians he thought might work well with Shania. Mutt already knew Shane; he had worked with him on the Bryan Adams album. He must have realized at that moment that David was proposing a band made up of musicians who had extensive experience with national recording acts. He was impressed with David's intuitive sense of the type of band that would best enhance Shania's sound.

In mid-June, a little over two months after the ad ran in *Metroland*, David's "dream band" was ready to audition for Mutt and Shania. Pulling the band together had proven harder than he'd expected. Some of the musicians he had contacted were on the road touring with other bands, and then there was the scheduling challenge of getting Mutt and Shania in the same country at the same time. But finally, all the calls had come together, and the group assembled at Sweetfish Recording Studio in Argyle, New York. The final configuration was Gary Burke, Graham Maby, Shane Fontayne, Allison Cornell, Mark Muller (pedal steel guitar), Phil Skyler (keyboards) and David. The group had rehearsed the day before at the studio, and had worked up three songs from *The Woman in Me*: "Any Man of Mine," "Whose Bed Have Your Boots Been Under?" and "The Woman in Me."

The day of the rehearsal, Mutt drove from Michael Bolton's house in Connecticut and Shania arrived, almost out of breath, directly from the airport following a flight out of England. After the perfunctory greetings and introductions, it was time to play. Mutt sat near the far wall of the studio, leaning forward, his head close to his knees, to listen. Shania sat on a stool, facing the band, microphone in hand. The band kicked into "Any Man of Mine," and the tight wall of sound almost overwhelmed the small studio. Shania sang tentatively at first, then gained momentum as she warmed up. The band hammered the ending, and Shania reacted with a delighted squeal, obviously pleased with the arrangement. "That was great," she said, laughing, and the band responded with its own round of laughter. "You'll have to excuse me," she continued, "I had to laugh." She reassured them, "I'm not laughing at you." The chanteuse had connected with the band.

The next song up was "Whose Bed Have Your Boots Been Under?" and Shania giggled at the innovative ending the band had worked up. Suddenly, she seemed to realize the level of musicianship that she was performing with. As if rising to the challenge, she used the next song to impress the band with her talent, and proceeded to deliver a devastating, emotional take on "The Woman in Me." When the song ended, there was almost total silence in the room, and then Shania said, "Terrific. Great. You play very well together."

The audition over, Shania began to express her expectations of both her career and a band. Her first statement was that she and Mutt weren't sure if the album would be accepted by Nashville, and subsequently, country radio.

*The Woman in Me* was her second album, and they'd taken some musical risks, but they were happy with it. "I'm never going to win any awards," Shania modestly mentioned to David after the audition. After thank yous and more compliments, Mutt and Shania left the studio.

Five days later Sheri left a message on David's answering machine: "Shania loves you guys and wants to use you." The Shania Twain Band was born. (Mutt and Shania had made the decision not to use Phil Skyler on keyboards, but instead recruited Eric Lambier, an old friend of theirs from Ontario.)

A week later, Mary Bailey called David and invited him to join Allison, Eric Lambier and Randy Thomas (from Shania's Nashville contingency of musicians) on a one-week promotional tour of the United Kingdom.

Shania's appearances in Scotland and England were not intended to build fans there. In fact, the three performances were at private showcases for music and media industry representatives in Great Britain. Shania and Mutt both felt that their music had international potential, and this was their first attempt at breaking into a market outside of Canada and the United States.

In July 1995, there were few people in London who had ever heard of Shania Twain. Back in the U.S. and Canada, the *Woman in Me* CD and her second single, "Any Man of Mine," were still a few weeks away from reaching the number one spot on *Billboard*'s Top Country Albums and Hot Country Singles charts. And while Shania's videos were shown on Country Music Television Europe, the country genre is not as widely listened to in England as it is in the United States or Canada.

The third performance of the tour took place at a trendy underground nightclub on London's south side, the last place that you'd expect to find an American country singer and her band. Though it was a bright, summer afternoon, it could have been 1 A.M. at Venom, the catacomb-like club where Shania was making her London debut. The hip, nose-ringed staff were scurrying about, preparing for today's unlikely guest of honor at a private showcase performance.

But there was a charged atmosphere among the invited guests at the afternoon showcase. It seemed like everyone from the Polydor, the London-based affiliate of Mercury, Shania's record label, were there—from the president on down to the interns. The audience was also teeming with representatives of the British entertainment media and British radio. Though most hadn't even heard of Shania Twain before that day, they all knew about her husband, Robert John "Mutt" Lange, the British record producer and songwriter who was closely associated with mega-stars Bryan Adams, Michael Bolton, and Def Leppard. Many were at Venom that day out of respect for Lange.

Shania and her band—David on lead guitar, Randy on guitar, Allison on fiddle and Eric on keyboards—planned to play four songs that day. The band had only been together for two other shows, in Glasgow and Manchester earlier that week, but they were all seasoned musicians, having played with other major country and rock bands in the past, and a sense of confidence emanated from the stage.

Shania launched her set that afternoon with unbridled enthusiasm. She opened with "Any Man of Mine," her

female-centric anthem that was destined to endear her to
millions of women fans, followed by the jaunty two-
stepping "Whose Bed Have Your Boots Been Under?".

The audience responded to the songs with encouraging,
but reserved, applause. The songs, after all, were not your
typical American country fare, and Shania was not your
typical country chanteuse. She had attitude, both lyrically
and musically, and the discerning audience took its time
in evaluating whether or not it thought Shania was a con-
tender for international acclaim.

Shania, a veteran of more than twenty years of performing live, knew instinctively how to build a musical set to
a theatrical climax. After charging the atmosphere with two
upbeat, swinging tunes, she chose the title song off *The
Woman in Me* to showcase her sultry, passionate side. The
band eased into the song, but after only a few bars, Shania
abruptly stopped the music. "Someone's out of tune," she
announced, turning toward the band. The shaking musicians immediately checked their tuning (even the pianist).
The audience's attention was riveted to the stage as they
sat on the edge of their seats waiting to see what Shania
Twain would do next. It was a very tense musical moment.

The problem was discovered and corrected, and the
band settled into the quiet, magical groove of the song. In
an emotional performance, Shania let each word soar, her
phrasing simply breathtaking. The audience responded
with an unrestrained round of applause. Shania had them
in the palm of her hand.

In what could have been seen as the sign of a tempera-
mental singer, her stopping the music ultimately revealed
Shania to be a musician who was clearly in control, and

one who accepted nothing less than musical perfection for herself and her audience.

Shania closed the set that afternoon with "(If You're Not in It for Love) I'm Outta Here," which met with a warm response from the audience. They were eager for more, but few people in the audience realized that the band was so new that it had only worked up the four songs it had just played.

Shania then remembered the closing cut on her CD, "God Bless the Child." It was a song that she wrote shortly after her parents died, and it resonates with a quiet sereneness and poignancy. She sang it a cappella, and her voice reached up to the heavens.

The British music elite had come to Venom that day to listen to a new country artist from Nashville with the famous British producer-husband. But few left the dark, underground club without the conviction that Shania Twain was unquestionably going to be a major force in country music in the years ahead. What they may not have realized until much later, as her CD began a two-year streak of hits and record-breaking sales, is that they had just seen the future of country music.

When Shania and her band returned to the United States, *The Woman in Me* was within spitting distance of the number one spot on the *Billboard* Top Country Albums chart. And her second single, "Any Man of Mine," was racing up the Hot Country Singles chart on a parallel course.

The band was about to be initiated on national television on one of the highest-rated talk shows in the country—*The Tonight Show with Jay Leno*. David and Shania barely had time to pack clean clothes after the UK shows before they were on their way to California.

Despite the heavy rotation that CMT was giving her second video, Shania and David traveled in relative obscurity. She arrived at the Albany airport alone, casually dressed in jeans and sneakers and wearing a black hat sporting the words "Bad Hair Day."

The day of *The Tonight Show,* the core band, augmented by additional musicians and singers, got together to rehearse. At the NBC studios, Kevin Lane, a publicist for Mercury Nashville, dropped by to inform the band that "Any Man of Mine" had just gone to number one on the *Billboard* charts. Shania, dressed in the same torn denim jeans and short vest that she wore in her video, delivered a confident performance, and the studio audience loved her.

Later, Shania and her newly minted band got together for dinner. Shania, in a particularly gregarious mood, pulled out her wedding pictures to show a few people at the table. She also revealed that she wore hair extensions, and that her real name was not Shania. It was a warm, friendly evening. There was a sense of camaraderie between Shania and her band. When the meal was over, she gave everyone a hug. It would be one of the first and only times that Shania would hang out with the band after a performance.

Less than a week later, Allison, David and Shania arrived at ABC studios for a taping of *Live! . . . With Regis & Kathie Lee.* They were scheduled to perform an acoustic version of "Any Man of Mine" that morning at 7 A.M. During a brief rehearsal, Shania experienced a problem keeping her guitar in tune, and commented on how much she admired David's black Gibson J-200. The next day, David called Gibson artist relations rep Jimmy Archey in New York. Shania would soon be the surprised owner of her own complimentary Gibson J-200.

Two days after Shania's thirtieth birthday, she performed at a Mercury radio program director's showcase in the Ritz Carlton Hotel ballroom in Laguna Beach, California. Backed by David, Allison, Eric and Dan Schafer (a Nashville musician who became a regular with the band), Shania performed "Whose Bed Have Your Boots Been Under?", "The Woman in Me," "Any Man of Mine" and "(If You're Not in It for Love) I'm Outta Here."

When the band members were handed their room list at the posh hotel, they noticed an unfamiliar name on the top of the list—Eilleen Lange. Shania's true identity, until this moment a secret, had now been revealed.

During the few weeks leading up to the August 30 show at Laguna Beach, David had been on the phone talking to Gillie Crowder at Mary Bailey's office arranging the details for the upcoming tour and rehearsals. The plan was for the band to live at Mutt and Shania's house in upstate New York and rehearse during October, November and January. Then they would hit the road as the opening act for, or possibly on a double bill with, either Neal McCoy or Wynonna in February.

With the band onstage at the Ritz Carlton, about to kick into its set, Mercury Nashville president Luke Lewis got up to introduce his "favorite singer" and her band and to make the announcement that Shania had just turned down a lucrative tour with Wynonna in order to concentrate on her next album. The announcement stunned the audience of country radio programmers. The band members, who had all been recruited with the expectation of touring with Shania, were the last ones to find out that the next year of their musical careers had just been canceled. Like the true professionals that they were, the band turned out a strong performance, but after the show, it was hard for them to mask their disappointment at the unexpected, and inappropriately timed, announcement.

Shania's decision not to tour was to become a controversial topic in Nashville that year. Many considered her decision a sign that she didn't have the talent to perform live and that Mutt had used studio magic to enhance her vocal abilities. Shania told the media that she didn't feel that one album of material was enough to support a full concert. This explanation, however, would only have been valid if she planned on headlining her own concert tour; as an opening act, an album of twelve tunes, including four number one hits, was more than adequate. The dilemma had become not whether she could carry a concert, but who would be appropriate for her to tour with. Most acts that were considered, including Wynonna and Garth Brooks, were already established, top-selling acts. They weren't about to let a relative newcomer who was blocking their attempts at controlling the *Billboard* charts open for them. And egos being what they are in Nashville, a shared billing would not have served any major artist, except for Shania.

The truth was, the album was enjoying such phenomenal sales, and her singles hitting number one with such regularity, that touring seemed almost pointless. If heavy rotation on country radio and video channels, almost monthly television appearances and meet-and-greet fan events at malls (which were drawing 20,000 people or more) could sustain *The Woman in Me*, why bother with a grueling, high-maintenance North American tour? Mutt and Shania made their choices, and while her loyal core band was disappointed at the lost opportunity, it was show business, after all.

Three weeks later, it was business as usual for the Shania Twain Band. They were heading north for a high-profile gig—the opening of General Motors Place, a major new entertainment complex in Vancouver, Canada. By now, Shania-mania was in full throttle. She had three singles overlapping on the charts (her third song and first ballad, *The Woman in Me*, was released in August), and the album had parked itself at the top of the *Billboard* Top Country Albums chart, with no plans on moving over.

Limousines picked up and drove Shania and her band to the immense GM Place (which doubles as home to the NBA's Vancouver Grizzlies), where Sarah McLachlan, Michelle Wright, David Foster, Jordan Hill, Blue Rodeo, Bass is Base and a bevy of professional skaters were also performing. The response to Shania's performance from the sold-out crowd of 25,000 was phenomenal. Shania was clearly a national treasure in her home country.

It had been three months since the band first came together, and while the configuration of the players changed from show to show, Shania's involvement in the band's "look" became a regular part of getting ready for a performance. The musicians got used to Shania's habit of choosing their stage clothes prior to the show. They would each bring a couple of outfits as options, and Shania would visit the dressing room selecting the clothes that either worked with what she was wearing or complimented the song they were showcasing.

Shania frequently opted for basic black for the band and a contrasting color for herself. More frequently, however, she dressed for stage in the identical outfit that she'd worn in one of her videos. Although it created a visual link to her video persona, wearing her video outfit onstage came across as more of a cliché than a fashion statement.

Still, she had come a long way from her first few gigs in the UK earlier that summer, when she had worn a pair of square-looking stretchy black pants with a sewn-in crease up the front.

One of the most high-profile television performances a singer can aspire to is the *Late Show with David Letterman*. The jokes about the frigid conditions at the Ed Sullivan Theater in New York, where the Letterman show is taped, are true. Shania appeared twice on the show—once on October 2, 1995, and again on February 26, 1996, both times in near subarctic conditions.

On her first appearance, backed by Allison, David, Dan, Eric Horner and the CBS Orchestra, Shania sang "(If You're Not in It for Love) I'm Outta Here." A few days before the show, Paul Schaffer called David to go over the arrangement of the song together. Paul, a consummate professional, had really done his musical homework. The accompaniment of the CBS Orchestra was a musical highlight for Shania's band.

Interestingly enough, Shania chose not to perform the single on *Letterman* that could have most benefited from the exposure—"The Woman in Me." The title track from her CD, released in mid-August, was slowly climbing the Hot Country Singles chart (it would eventually peak at number 14 on November 4, 1995). The *Late Show* might have helped nudge the song a few spots higher, considering it was still ascending when the show aired.

"If You're Not in It for Love," on the other hand, was six weeks away from debuting on the charts. It would eventually reach the number one spot in February 1996.

Shania's second appearance on the *Late Show with David Letterman*, in late February, 1996, coincided with the debut of "You Win My Love" on the charts. The song was destined to reach number one in early May.

Shania performed at her first awards show, the *Billboard* Music Awards, on December 6, 1995, at the Coliseum in New York City. It was her first experience playing at an event that not only featured a mixed bag of musical genres, but was a virtual who's who of the American music scene. Also on the bill that night were Hootie and the Blowfish, Stevie Wonder, Michael Bolton, Goo Goo Dolls, Tina Turner and Al Green. If the pop and rock world hadn't heard of Shania yet, it was going to have a hard time avoiding her that night.

Shania, backed by David, Gary, Graham, Allison, Dan, Chris Rodriguez, Mark Muller and Russ Taff, was one of the only artists scheduled to perform her song live ("If You're Not in It for Love").

The day before at rehearsal, Jimmy Archey from Gibson Guitars had presented Shania with her own J-200, the model that David owned that she'd admired at the *Live! . . . With Regis & Kathie Lee* show. It was a gorgeous instrument, and Shania loved it. Another memorable moment at the awards show took place during the sound check. Shania and the band noticed a woman in the front row who was rockin' out in her seat. She was swaying and grooving, her hair flying around crazily. When the song ended, it became apparent to the band that the woman was Tina Turner. David walked over to Gary, who was still behind his drums, and said, "If Tina thinks we've got a groove, that's got to be the highest authority!"

Close to two months would go by before David was asked to get the band together again for a show. In the time between the *Billboard* Music Awards in December 1995 and the American Music Awards on January 30, 1996, Shania's career went through a major transition—Mary Bailey, her loyal and hardworking manager of four years, was fired.

Most Nashville insiders were not surprised by the news. If Mary's strength as a manager was her unwavering dedication to Shania, her weakness was her inexperience orchestrating the complex and demanding career of a country superstar. Sadly, when Shania ended her professional relationship with Mary, she also lost one of her oldest and dearest friends. A few months after Mary was let go as Shania's manager, they crossed paths again. At the 1996 Canadian Country Music awards, Mary was presented with the Manager of the Year award. It was a not-so-subtle commentary from the Canadian country music industry that they recognized Mary's profound impact on building Shania's career, even if Shania had apparently forgotten.

While some expected Shania to announce a high-powered replacement, she instead took on the day-to-day operations of her band and career with the help of her assistant Sheri Thorn and former Mary Bailey Management

Shania rehearses for her 1998 international concert tour. Nashville, Tennessee.

Shania with President Bill Clinton at the Ford Center in 1996. Washington, D.C.

A promotional photo of eighteen-year-old Eilleen Twain in 1983. Timmins, Ontario.

(Country Music News)

On stage at Fan
Fair 1996.
Nashville,
Tennessee.

(Blanchard/Porter,
Country Music News)

At a celebrity baseball
game at Fan Fair 1996.
Nashville, Tennessee.

(Blanchard/Porter, Country
Music News)

Shania receiving an RIAA plaque in 1996 for sales of 7 million copies of *The Woman in Me*. Nashville, Tennessee.

(Blanchard/Porter, Country Music News)

Shania at the 1996 Juno
Awards ceremony in
Canada. Halifax, Nova
Scotia.

(Blanchard/Porter, Country Music
News)

Demonstrating her expertise with a chain saw on TNN's *Prime Time Country* in 1998. Nashville, Tennessee.

(© Phill Snel/Maclean's)

Shania at the Macy's Thanksgiving Day Parade in 1995. New York, New York.

(© Peter Bregg/Maclean's)

A skating expedition at Rockefeller Center, 1995. New York, New York.

(© Peter Bregg/Maclean's)

At Rockefeller Center on a promotional visit to New York in 1995. New York, New York.

(© Peter Bregg/Maclean's)

publicist Patty Lou Andrews. The three worked as a "management group," seeing to the business, performing and promotional aspects of Shania's career.

The American Music Awards, held at the Shrine Auditorium in Los Angeles, was Shania's first booking as a self-managed artist. The awards conveniently coincided, almost to the day, with the arrival of "(If You're Not in It for Love) I'm Outta Here" on the top of the Hot Country Singles chart. Once again, Shania and her band were among the few who were booked to perform live at the show (most acts performed with recorded tracks, nonamped instruments and, in many cases, lip-synched vocals).

Two other monster country music artists performed at the AMAs in 1996—Reba McEntire and Garth Brooks. It's hard to guess what these country veterans thought about Shania, considering that she had owned the number one spot on the *Billboard* Top Country Albums chart for twenty-nine weeks breaking Reba's record.

The performance, one of Shania's best of the year, was memorable for more than her strong vocal performance. It was the show at which Shania stunned almost every country music fan in North America by wearing the most amazing skintight black vinyl pants, halter top and spike heels. It's safe to say that no other female country artist had ever dressed so anticountry! Perhaps in a sudden blush of modesty, Shania had added a textured, waist-length green jacket over the outfit. The jacket clearly looked like a last-minute addition aimed at making the devastating outfit look less risqué.

Shania-mania was in full swing at that performance. The roar of the crowd was deafening after Sinbad introduced

Shania and the band: Gary, Graham, David, Mark, Russ, Dan, Chris and Allison. The performance came across as more rock 'n' roll than country. Shania even cued the band backstage with the comment, "Rock this world!"

About a month later, Shania picked up a 1996 Block-buster Entertainment Award at the Pantages Theatre in Los Angeles. She also debuted a new song on national television, "You Win My Love," which was destined to be her third number one hit in less than a year. David, long since designated as the bandleader, had brought together the usual crew—himself, Gary, Hugh, Allison, Mark, Dan, Chris and Hugh MacDonald—to back Shania (Graham was out on tour with They Might Be Giants, and Hugh, Bon Jovi's bass player, filled in).

Shania had just been featured on the cover of *Los Angeles* magazine, and it seemed to the band, and possibly everyone else at the theater that day, that Shania was everywhere.

Almost every live performance that Shania and her band did was limited to one song. For musicians used to national concert tours, it must have seemed like the performances were over in the blink of an eye. In June 1996, Shania and her musicians finally had an opportunity to show the world that they could handle a set of music, and not simply one tune. Shania was headlining, for the first time in the four years that she had participated, Mercury Nashville's showcase at Fan Fair '96 (the spot that Billy Ray Cyrus had dominated since his runaway hit "Achy Breaky Heart" in 1993). It would turn out to be one of the most difficult performances of her career.

David and Shania had brought together a stellar group

of musicians for Fan Fair, which was held at the Tennessee State Fairgrounds: Gary, Graham, Allison, Mark, Dan, Chris, David, Will Owlsley, Terry McMillian, Mark W. Winchester and Steve Dudash.

The band rehearsed their five-song set, which included "Any Man of Mine," "Home Ain't Where His Heart Is (Anymore)," "You Win My Love," "No One Needs to Know" and "(If You're Not in It for Love) I'm Outta Here" at Soundcheck, in the Nashville industrial area. A sign posted on the door of the warehouse-sized studio read "Closed Rehearsal."

Behind the door, however, the atmosphere was almost family-like. At the back of the room, Sheri and Patty Lou, Shania's management team, were holding court on comfortable couches, working on promotional and logistical strategies. Dave Baughn, Shania's longtime production manager and soundman, ruled from the soundboard. David had his hands full keeping track of the eleven musicians (twelve including Shania) and trying to concentrate on his own musical role as lead guitarist. Amidst all the buzz of conversation and musical activity, Shania's companion and security dog, Tim, lay patiently in a corner, relaxed but alert.

Shania was very focused and exacting during rehearsals, undoubtedly anticipating the need to put on her best performance to date for the media, industry reps and fans who would fill the stadium a few days later. She kept checking the tempo of the songs (she prefers to play her songs slightly faster live) and even went around and listened to each individual guitar amp. By the second day, things were coming together, and Shania was clearly pleased with the sound.

It had rained the first day of Fan Fair '96, but on Tuesday afternoon, the day of the Mercury Nashville showcase, the sun was blazing. Backstage is always a hornet's nest of activity—dozens of radio, record and media representatives are milling around (even PolyGram head Danny Goldberg was on hand for the show), eating the free food and beverages and absorbing the true flavor of country music at its most raucous. Immediately following Billy Ray Cyrus's performance, the wings of the stage became jammed. It was the moment everyone was waiting for— Shania's only live concert performance of 1996. There were few at Fan Fair, whether industry members, the media or fans, who wanted to miss this historic occasion, in which Miss Twain would prove or disprove her ability to perform live in concert. Shania, after all, was the biggest thing in country music in 1996.

Fan Fair's showcases take place in the Tennessee State Fair Ground's outdoor stadium. Two full stages are set up, and bands go on back-to-back, with never more than a five-minute gap between acts. All day long, for five days straight, 24,000 fans are treated to almost nonstop country music. It isn't surprising that the $90 tickets sell out weeks before the event each year.

The sun was blazing down directly on the stage when emcee Sammy Kershaw introduced Shania. It was her cue to give the band, via their linked earphones, the signal to kick into "Any Man of Mine." What should have been a split-second pause between the introduction and the start of the song turned into a nerve-racking delay. The band waited for Shania to give it the vocal cue to start the song. It was then that everyone realized that Shania's ear monitors (a higher-tech version of floor monitors) were not working. In an instant, sound technicians raced onto the stage and began checking wires. The fans, realizing that there were technical problems onstage, waited patiently in the oppressive 90-degree heat.

When the technicians were unable to correct the problem, Shania realized that she would have to begin her set with or without their assistance. Luckily, the stadium sound system and the band's monitors were not affected— any music produced onstage would project into the audience as planned. It was Shania's lifeline—her ear monitor— that was not working, making it difficult for her to hear the blend of her voice and the band's instrumentation. She would have to rely on the stadium's front speakers, twenty feet in front of her, to determine that they were all playing in synch.

Though it was far from ideal technically, Shania knew there was no option but to perform. She motioned to the band members to start, and as though they'd played a hundred concerts with Shania, they fell into an extended intro to "Any Man of Mine." When Shania arrived on the stage, dressed in black leather pants, a matching vest and short white shirt, the audience exploded.

Once the band started playing, no one would have guessed that there were serious technical problems onstage. The audience was enthusiastic, cheering loudly at the end of each song. "You Win My Love" quickly followed "Any Man of Mine," its infectious hook and ascending key change upping the energy level even more. Then Shania slowed it down for her ballad. It was as if the audience held its collective breath during the first verse of

"Home Ain't Where His Heart Is (Anymore)." Shania then picked up a guitar for a bright rendition of "No One Needs to Know." The band pulled out the stops with a rockin', high-energy take of "(If You're Not in It for Love) I'm Outta Here." Though the audience was clearly enraptured by Shania's performance, the applause quickly died out after her final song, and the throngs left the stadium without calling for an encore.

The performance had been a critical success, despite its precarious start. Shania had proven her doubters wrong. Not only could she excel onstage, both musically and vocally, but she had handled a difficult technical problem with the grace of the veteran musician that she was.

There was never an explanation for the technical problems that Shania and her band encountered at Fan Fair '96. One sound technician suggested that a wireless feed operated by a television camera crew may have inadvertently jammed the sound system onstage.

On August 28, 1996, Shania performed for the last time with her "band." Her appearance on *Late Night with Conan O'Brien* managed to squeeze a bit more life out of her *Woman in Me* album, which had already sold eight million copies and produced six hits, but which was clearly beginning to show signs of overexposure. Her most recent single, "No One Needs to Know," had peaked at number one several weeks earlier, and two future releases, "Home Ain't Where His Heart Is (Anymore)" and "God Bless the Child," would not rise above number 28 and number 48, respectively.

The band had sensed that things were beginning to wind down and that Shania would need to turn her attention to the studio if she wanted to release a new album in 1997.

That final performance on Conan O'Brien's late-night show at NBC studios in New York featured Gary, Graham, Hugh, Mark, Will, David and Ed Roynesdal (Allison was on tour with Pat Benatar). Shania played her Gibson J-200 for the first time on television. It was an honest, bright performance.

Shania did, however, perform again in 1996, at the Country Music Association's awards show in Nashville in October. She debuted an extended version of "God Bless the Child," which was to be her eighth single off the album (the extended version was released as the single), with one of American's finest gospel groups, Take Six, backing her.

Except for receiving a Christmas card in 1996 from Shania, and 1099 tax forms from Twain Zone, David was never contacted again by Shania or her management team to call the band back together. Though the band had only come together every month or so to rehearse and perform between June 1995 and August 1996, it had nonetheless become a musically tight, cohesive group.

In the fall of 1997, a few members of Shania's 1995–96 band contacted Jon Landau, now Shania's manager, to find out what the plans were for bringing the New York band together for television dates and rehearsals for the concert tour. Jan Stabile, an assistant at Jon Landau Management, expressed surprise at the queries. She wasn't aware, she said, that Shania even had a band. She suggested that the musicians submit their resumes for consideration. A few musicians did, but some refused, feeling insulted by the slight.

Most members of her band, however, were not so naive that they expected to be rehired after a year of inactivity.

But there was still some disappointment among the ranks. After all, many of them had been initially hired to go on a tour to support *The Woman in Me* that never took place. Many members of the band had operated under the assumption that they were still considered "Shania's band," even after the *Conan* performance in August 1996, and that a future live concert tour in 1997 or 1998 was still a possibility.

When Shania began her search for a new band in late 1997 to take on tour in support of her third album, *Come on Over*, she must have reflected back on the talent and dedication of her New York band, and realized how amazing their live shows had been. Though she could have simply hired them for the 1998 tour, she decided to begin with a clean slate. There were two exceptions—Allison, on fiddle and keyboards, and Mark, on steel guitar, were offered spots in the new band.

It was a year earlier, in November 1996, that Shania had announced that she had signed a management contract with Jon Landau Management. Jon, who spent his early twenties writing about the detonating rock scene for *Rolling Stone* and other publications, had begun a twenty-year affiliation with Bruce Springsteen in the 1970s, as his coproducer and manager. His company, which he owns with Barbara Carr, handles only three acts: Bruce Springsteen, Natalie Merchant and Shania. Landau has his fingers in other projects, including coproducing the 1998 film *Titanic* with writer-director James Cameron.

Jon Landau's impressive power within the music industry cannot be overestimated. His tentacles extend to the record, publishing and movie industries, and Shania could either find herself riding the crest of an international multimedia career or alienating her audience by growing completely out of touch with her musical roots. Mutt, who has been intimately involved in many levels of Shania's career for the past five years, has a lot in common with his wife's manager. Jon Landau, a veteran of the recording studio, has produced albums by Jackson Browne and Bruce Springsteen.

The real question is whether Shania will be able to assert her ideas now that her career is dominated by a major artist management company. Perhaps the answer can be found in a comment that Kevin Lane, director of media relations at Mercury Nashville, once made. "Shania has the best instincts of anyone I have ever met. She knows exactly what is best for her."

Shania's intuitive nature, however, did not seem to be too concerned about the feelings of several people who helped get her where she is today, and who were subsequently and unceremoniously "released." To some it seemed that Shania turned her back on several loyal team players: manager Mary Bailey, publicist Patty Lou Andrews, the musicians who played with her in 1995 and 1996, long-time keyboard player Eric Lambier and production manager and sound technician Dave Baughn. Even her makeup artist, Jill Sokolee, who Shania first worked with in Canada in the early 1990s, wasn't listed on the credits of Shania's CD *Come on Over*. In fact, Mercury Nashville doesn't even rate on her third CD. Its parent company, Mercury Records (a division of PolyGram), now gets top billing as her label.

Perhaps one reason for her apparently jaded attitude toward her associates is rooted in Shania's fiercely independent and pragmatic approach to business. After all, this is a woman who at twenty-two took on the full responsibility of raising three siblings and settling her parents' estate. She no doubt has a sensitive side, but when it comes to getting things done, her motto might as well be, "Only the toughest survive."

Celebrity has also had a profound effect on Shania's ability to control her environment. She is an admitted "control freak," and her fame has stifled her love of freedom. As a child, Shania has said, she had more independence than she has now.

As 1997 came to a close, Shania again found herself, briefly, in the city that had once claimed all of her dreams—Nashville. Her appearance on the Country Music Association awards show almost didn't take place. The performance spots on the internationally televised show are almost always reserved for nominees; being one of country music's biggest events of the year, it's only fair that the performers who are contenders get the coveted performance spots. In 1997, however, two female artists with forthcoming album releases, neither of whom were in the running for CMA awards, wanted the exposure of performing on the awards show. And the CMA, not oblivious to the ratings war, decided to give in to the pressure. Consequently, Shania and Wynonna both launched singles ("Love Gets Me Every Time" and "When Love Starts Talking," respectively) on the show.

Ironically, Shania, who has collected almost every other music award in the world, has never had a CMA award bestowed on her by her peers—the Nashville music industry. Her presence on the show must have been particularly annoying to those who had traveled more traditional routes to earn their spot on the broadcast, which, after all, is intended to honor Nashville's favorite sons and daughters for their unwavering loyalty to preserving the traditional roots of country music. The awards are given to those musicians whose music respects and pays tribute to the giants of country music—George Jones, Merle Haggard, Loretta Lynn, Hank Williams and others. Over the past decade or so, more and more country artists, like Shania, have begun to veer off the path of the "great ones," allowing country music's purest strains to be diluted into hybrid styles that cross over into the world of pop and rock. And every year Nashville asserts its power by rewarding those who are true to their roots, and chastising those who have strayed too far from the flock.

A year earlier, almost to the day, at the 1996 CMA awards, the question on everyone's mind was whether Shania Twain's phenomenal success with *The Woman in Me* CD would get the nod or the cold shoulder from Nashville. When she failed to be called to the podium to accept any of the three awards she was nominated for, her fans throughout America and Canada watched in disbelief.

She left behind a message, however. Shania performed an expanded version of "God Bless the Child," the musical tribute to her parents that she wrote soon after they died in 1987. On the CMA show that year, she performed it accompanied by Take Six. The song, powerful in its message, became almost an anthem with the addition of the richly textured vocals of the gospel group. Near the end of the song, a choir of children of every nationality joined

Shania and Take Six onstage. When the song was over, the audience sat in utter silence for a moment. Shania had veered off the traditional country path again, and this time it was in front of the biggest group of country purists in the music business.

It's hard to say what the Nashville insiders in the auditorium were thinking of Shania's performance at that moment, but for the millions of viewers watching her on television, country music would never be the same again.

## CHAPTER SEVEN

# FROM PYRAMIDS TO ROADSIDE CAFE

*Anyone with any sense at all has found a shaded spot to escape the blazing midsummer sun. In this desert, on the outskirts of Cairo, the temperature is over 100, and still it is business as usual for the soda vendors and camel owners who cater to the tourists who have traveled from around the world to see the Great Pyramids. Today the sun is particularly oppressive, and even the horses are leaning against the stone fences in the narrow band of shade that offers some relief.*

*Shania is sitting on a low chair against the side of the trailer that the crew is using during the shooting of "The Woman in Me" video. The ice in the drink that was handed to her minutes before has melted, but she continues to sip the liquid to avoid dehydration.*

*"We're ready to shoot the scene with you on the horse, Shania," the director's assistant says to her. "Do you think you*

*can handle the heat out there? We're going to try to get the shot
as quickly as possible."*

*"No, I'll be okay. I'm just worried about the horses," she an-
swers, concern in her voice.*

*"That is not a problem," the young horse handler says to her
as he leads the chestnut Arabian gelding over to Shania so that
she can mount it. "These horses are here ever day, in every con-
dition. They are used to it."*

*He gives Shania a leg up and helps her adjust the stirrups.
The white cotton dress and streaming veil that she is wearing in
this shot move slightly as a faint breeze stirs the air. Suddenly,
the horse veers to the right after catching a glimpse of the moving
veil out of the corner of its eye. Shania's foot strikes the edge of
the stone fence that they are standing near, and a sharp pain
runs through her leg. She pulls back expertly on the reins and
speaks slowly to the horse. "It's okay, boy," she whispers. He is
breathing shallowly, and she can see the red of his nostrils as
they flare open as if searching for the source of the wind.*

*The horse handler rushes over and takes the reins in his hand.
"Your costume frightened him," he said. "Are you all right?"*

*"Great. Fine. I just need to cover up this cut on my ankle."
Someone appears with a first aid kit. Within a few minutes, the
shooting session begins.*

*Shania is led toward the base of the Pyramids. She is surprised
that the sand-colored monuments seem so much smaller than she
remembers them from photos. Even the nearby Sphinx seems di-
minutive. Shania is nonetheless captivated by the magic of this
place—the turbaned men in their cotton robes, the overpowering
sense of history and mystery, the noble lineage of the Arabian
horse that she is riding.*

*In a moment, the cameras will be in place to shoot her scene and she will gallop her horse down the cracked sand road between the Pyramids and the edge of the visitors' compound. The sun beats down relentlessly on Shania and her horse, the way it has done in this part of the world since before the time of the pharaohs. She squeezes her legs against the horse slightly, and he responds to her expert horsemanship. They break into a gallop, the hard, dry wind on their faces as they cross the desert.*

◆　◆　◆

Shania Twain is a classic case of how influential music videos have become in breaking new country artists, expanding their popularity and impacting on their worldwide record sales. There is little question that Shania has benefited from the exposure of her videos on country music cable stations, but it is also true that her daring and diverse video clips have had a powerful impact on audience growth for stations like TNN and CMT. Shania's enormous popularity among rock and pop music fans has drawn many of them over to the world of country music television, if only for a browse. Many of these visitors have stayed and become fans of both country music and country videos.

Shania released three music videos from her debut CD *Shania Twain*, eight from *The Woman in Me* and an anticipated ten for *Come on Over*. All of them are timed for release to support and promote the corresponding single on radio.

It's only been in the past fifteen years that music videos have become a standard component of a recording artist's career. Prior to that, artists vied for coveted performances

on variety shows, awards programs and late night talk
shows if they wanted their fans to catch a glimpse of them
outside of concert halls or nightclubs.

Promotional video clips—fictional vignettes or live concert footage built around one song—had their roots in rock
'n' roll. As the expansion of cable television opened the
door for specialty channels, communications companies
recognized the potential for musical groups to promote
their albums by turning their songs into cinematic minidra-
mas. When MTV was launched in the early 1980s, most
rock and pop acts had never even contemplated the visual
aspect of their music. When MTV, with its hip, irreverent
veejays, began screening fast-action rock video clips twenty-
four hours a day, it became an instant hit with baby boomers and teens. Though many traditional-minded musicians
consider videos to be a crass commercialization of their
music, nowadays most bands begin conceiving video story
lines for their songs even before they are released in audio
format. Today, it is standard practice in the music industry
to release a promotional video whenever a single is released.

More than sixty years separates the introduction of the
two most powerful mediums in the history of country music—recorded music in the 1920s and the music video in
the 1980s. Records (now CDs and cassette tapes) and videos are instrumental in giving musicians, songwriters and
singers the means of transmitting their musical vision to
their audience. When linked with the mass-market tech-
nologies of commercial radio and cable television, records
and videos are capable of instantaneously reaching millions of listeners and viewers around the world.

Live concerts and variety music programs have been a
mainstay of television since it first went on the air in the

1940s. Dale Evans and Roy Rogers became American icons as much for their music as for their appearances on western television shows and specials. Hollywood hasn't overlooked the demand for country music–focused stories, either. Movies like *Coal Miner's Daughter* brought Loretta Lynn's life story to the big screen, and *Urban Cowboy* celebrated the lifestyle and music of citified country in the 1970s.

By 1983, the rock video experiment had proven itself viable, and other musical genres began taking a serious look at the concept of using video clips to promote their sound. That year country music got its own country version of MTV—The Nashville Network (TNN). Seven million cable subscribers had the opportunity to tune in to the premiere of TNN on March 7, 1983. The station was launched from two Nashville sets—the stage of the Grand Ole Opry House and the Stage Door Lounge at the Opryland Hotel. Ralph Emery was the emcee on TNN's inaugural night, and the Nashville Symphony was the "backup" band to the dozens of country stars who performed on the program. There were also live remotes from Chicago, Dallas, Denver, Los Angeles and New York. Ralph Emery went on to serve as the anchor of his own nightly music variety show on TNN, *Emery's Nashville Now*.

The "fathers" of TNN were E. W. Wendell, who was then the president of Opryland USA, and Tom Griscom, the corporation's vice president. Tom had also been the manager of WSM-TV, which was owned by the National Life and Accident Insurance Company, a major investor in broadcast and country music companies. The two men had a vision of a country music cable station that would not only promote artists and record labels, but also offer video production facilities. Cable was still a new industry in the United States, and the jury was out on whether it was a safe investment. Nevertheless, TNN was launched with an investment of fifty million dollars, and headquartered in Music City.

From the beginning, TNN was committed to the dual themes of country music and country lifestyles. On its musical side, the cable station offered country dance shows, live and taped nightclub and theater concerts, and music videos. On its lifestyles side, it programmed shows on motor sports, outdoor sports, cooking and crafts. In 1985, TNN began broadcasting portions of the Grand Ole Opry, and in 1991 it launched a music history series hosted by the Statler Brothers. With the growth of the cable industry, which is now available to most homes in Canada and the United States, TNN was reaching sixty-four million households by 1998.

TNN continues to maintain its focus on both country music and country life. Its regular NASCAR and NHRA (National Hot Rod Association) programs draw some of its biggest audiences. TNN also takes credit for breaking many of country music's biggest names, many of them inclined toward "traditional country." Die-hard fans will recall Randy Travis's first television appearance on TNN— he was working as a short-order cook at the Nashville Palace, and he took a break from the grill to sing on a country music special.

CMT, also launched in 1983, has played a significant role in the expansion and popularity of New Country. Its stations in Canada, the United States, Europe, the Pacific Rim and Latin America all offer the best of country, Country

Rock and Country Pop. The twenty-four-hour, all-video country music channel is the more progressive, hipper sister of TNN.

CMT's first foray into the world music market took place in 1992, when it launched a station in the United Kingdom. Before long, CMT was being seen in a number of European countries. In 1994, it entered the Asia-Pacific region, and in 1995, CMT started a cable station in Latin America. In total, CMT is available in fifty-five countries and territories, and is broadcast in English, Spanish and Portuguese. In addition to programming Canadian and American country artists, each international outlet also airs videos by country artists from its own region. In the Latin American market, CMT also offers Tejano and other Spanish language music styles.

In 1997, CBS bought CMT (US) and TNN from Gaylord Entertainment Corporation (which still owns the Grand Ole Opry).

CMT (US) is also a shareholder in CMT Canada, as a result of a merger with the New Country Network (NCN) in 1995. NCN was launched as a rival to CMT, which had been broadcasting its American programming on Canadian cable systems for a few years. Shortly after NCN came into existence on January 1, 1995, its owners filed a complaint with the Canadian Radio and Television Commission (CRTC) to have the American-based CMT banned from Canadian cable systems. The owners of NCN claimed that the presence of the American-owned station on Canadian cable was not in compliance with federal broadcast and advertising protection laws designed to protect the Canadian broadcasting industry from foreign control. CMT retaliated by banning Canadian country acts, who were not signed to American labels, from airing on their American channel. Eventually, NCN and CMT formed a business partnership, whereby CMT (US) owns a 20 percent share of CMT Canada. The two services are managed and operated separately, and even the programming is different on each station, to reflect the diverse interests of the two distinct national audiences. Approximately 40 percent of the videos played on the Canadian CMT are by Canadian country acts, giving it a unique character all of its own.

Shania's videos have received strong support from both CMT and TNN; however, CMT's New Country format offers the closer fit for her style of music and videos.

Shania and Mutt have complete creative control over their musical recordings, but the same is not the case in music video productions. The songwriting duo rely heavily on the talent and intuition of leading music video producers and directors to conceive and artistically develop the visual interpretations of their songs. Shania, however, clearly plays a key role in interpreting and defining herself, or the characters that she portrays, in her videos. Some of the productions have become award-winning classics, while others have simply become interesting entries in the visual archives of her music.

The first video that Mutt saw Shania in, on CMT Europe in 1993, was "What Made You Say That." Taped in Miami, Florida, in January 1993, it was the first of five Twain clips masterminded by award-winning director Steven Goldmann for the Collective, a video production company. Goldmann was named 1996 and 1997 CMT video director of the year, with video credits that include Kathy Mattea's

"455 Rocket" and "I'm on Your Side," Pam Tillis's "All the Good Ones Are Gone" and Paul Brandt's "I Meant to Do That."

"What Made You Say That" looks like a fashion shoot for *Glamour* magazine. On an oddly deserted Florida beach, Shania goes through five outfit changes, from a funky black midriff-baring top and bell-bottom pants, to an elegant off-white body-clinging dress, to a pair of jeans and a tank top. She playfully dances around a bemused Chippendales-type model, who finally succeeds in rolling around in the waves with her. Meanwhile, when the song gets to the chorus, its words appear on the screen, like scrambled Disneyesque follow-the-bouncing-ball lyrics. Shania makes it clear that she is not only comfortable in front of the camera, but that the camera truly adores her.

Steven Goldmann returned for "You Lay a Whole Lot of Love on Me," the only song Shania ever released that did not crack *Billboard*'s Top 100 Country Singles charts. The video is another good reason that the song never had an impact on country music fans.

Taped in Montreal in August 1993, the video is a plodding romp through the streets of Montreal's beautiful historic district, cut with shots of Shania rolling around in a Laura Ashley–inspired hotel room pining away for her beau. She also plays the role of a lounge singer with enough makeup on to scare a baby. The male love interest arrives, running through the town's plaza with his suitcase, and alternates offering her a lift in a horse-drawn carriage and a classy convertible. The romantic ambience of the video is totally shattered when the guy appears in a baseball cap and a trench coat. The video obviously had no impact on the viability of the single on radio. It does give Shania some guidelines for what not to include in her future videos: big hair, guys in baseball caps and layers of makeup.

It isn't a surprise that director Sean Penn would create a minimovie for "Dance with the One That Brought You," which he directed in May 1993. Actor Charles Durning plays the good-time Charlie who arrives at a country music dance and immediately plops his wallflower wife at a table while he hits the dance floor. Shania is the girl singer in the band, and Charles doesn't leave her off the list of women he flirts with during the evening. The video flashes back to the 1940s, to a black-and-white scene which proves that history does repeat itself. The man in that scene has also dropped off the missus at the table, while he cruises the dance hall without his woman, played by Shania, to show off his fancy footwork. In both scenes, the man comes back to his patient wife for a slow dance. It's a charming story, and it confirmed that Shania would have been a knockout selling war bonds.

"Whose Bed Have Your Boots Been Under?" was the first video off Shania's second album, *The Woman in Me,* and it proved to be a 360-degree image transformation for her, orchestrated by the guru of goddesses, John Derek (who succeeded in a similar cinematic and visual metamorphosis for his wife, Bo, with the movie *10*). The actor-director-producer was initially a reluctant recruit to the Shania Twain reconstitution project, and finally agreed to shoot Shania's album photographs for *The Woman in Me* only after Bo cajoled him. Bo produced this video, with John in the director's chair, for their company, Crackerjack Films.

The Dereks' video was not the first attempt to create a promotional video for "Whose Bed Have Your Boots Been Under?". The first version was produced in England and featured animated boots. It was wisely rejected by Mercury Nashville, which then approached John and Bo to create one that would help break the album.

The fictional lead woman in this video clip delivers a cheeky, emasculating spin on the classic subject of infidelity. Rather than let herself be torn apart by a womanizing boyfriend, the singer brushes off the jerk. It's a defining moment in the creation of Shania's public persona—a woman who trades in the victim role for that of the victor. In the clip, Shania is the woman in red, slinking around a greasy spoon cafe cavorting with a group of working-class guys like the spirit of extramarital affairs past. The men are oblivious to the intruder, even while she dances on the tables, plays with their food and overpours a cup of coffee. Meanwhile, Shania is outside playing the spirit of wholesome country girls, strumming her guitar on a white-washed wood porch in Small Town USA. She is so appealingly fresh in her bare feet, acoustic guitar and minimal makeup that it makes her sexpot alter ego in the red dress seem absurd.

The comedic feel of the video was apparently lost on the committee that reviews clips for CMT in Nashville. They called the video redundant and too sexy. The predominantly female screening committee was clearly disturbed by the Dereks' interpretation of the song, which they mistook for an attempt to sexualize country music. If they had listened to the lyrics, they might have heard a story about female empowerment. While the song raced up the country single charts, CMT never put it into heavy rotation. TNN wouldn't even air the clip. It's difficult to say whether "Whose Bed Have Your Boots Been Under?" might have moved past its *Billboard* peak at number 11 if country video channels had supported it. That will never be known, but the shocking video—by country music standards, anyway—put Shania-watchers on red alert for her second release off *The Woman in Me.*

John and Bo Derek were back for a second time as director and producer of "Any Man of Mine." Part of the video was shot on location in Santa Ynez, California, in August 1994, with additional scenes added by another director, Charley Randazzo of Planet Pictures, in April 1995. Observant viewers will recognize the change in seasons in the video. The dusty cattle drive scene was shot in late summer, while the lush, green, pastoral shots where Shania is prancing in front of the wood wagon were obviously shot in early spring.

For some reason, the John Derek–directed version of the song did not work out completely. Charley was brought in to tape additional scenes and to edit the new version together. The outstanding results made country music history, and helped propel Shania's image to a new level.

The clip starts out with Shania competently riding a horse on a cattle drive. She looks impressive rounding up a herd of cattle and then loading up her own horse in a trailer before jumping behind the driver's seat of a high-test pickup truck. You can't help but be impressed. The transition from a cattle wrangler to a stable girl to a sophisticated woman in a black dress could be the story line for a perfume commercial. Shania's dancing scenes in front of the wagon, and in silhouette in the barn, give the un-mistaken impression that she is a singer who is comfortable with her body.

The video is a barrage of alluring scenes—the towel-grabbing, nose-kissing horse (who somehow manages to gain access to her bathroom), the blinding green pastoral scenes of Shania dancing and simply hanging out in the knee-high hay, and the spirited barn scenes, where she makes cleaning stalls seem almost a metaphysical experience.

The spunky video, and its flippant song that defined male-female relationships in the summer of '95, was one of the biggest hits of the year. By July 22, 1995, the album, song and video had all captured the number one spots in *Billboard* and on CMT and TNN.

The third single off *The Woman in Me* was positioned to break Shania in Europe. The marketing staff at PolyGram thought that a ballad set in a non-American setting might be the ticket to attract an older, international audience. The title track off her CD, ''The Woman in Me (Needs the Man in You),'' is a sensuous throwback to classic foreign films. Taped over a three-day period on location at the Pyramids outside of Cairo and at sites along the Nile, the video (or the song, for that matter) does not reveal its connection to a faraway place called Nashville. Directed by Markus Blunder of Uground, the clip is an exotic journey to another era and civilization that is rarely seen in a music video. Shot in the blazing sun, in temperatures that went above 100 degrees, the video was exhausting but exhilarating for Shania to make. If Mutt introduced her to the fascinating world of Europe, her music has opened her eyes to worlds that she only dreamed about in Timmins.

The dream-like scenes in the video are cinematically intriguing, and portray Shania in the unexpected role of a Sahara princess, complete with an entourage of ladies-in-waiting and sensual scenes set amongst the ancient pillars of a temple. She also had the chance to fulfill the dream of any horse-crazy girl—racing across the desert on an Arabian horse. In Shania's case, the riding scene resulted in an injury, though not a serious one. Her cut ankle was a small price to pay for the adventure. The final results propelled the video to the number one spot at CMT and to number 5 at TNN. The single peaked at number 14 on the *Billboard* Country Singles chart.

The Collective's Steven Goldmann returned to direct Shania's next three video releases—"(If You're Not in It for Love) I'm Outta Here," "You Win My Love," and "No One Needs to Know."

One interesting bit of trivia from the set of "I'm Outta Here" deals with the skintight black pants that Shania wears in the video. It took a reported five hours for a seamstress to fit the pants to Shania's specifications. There are no reports on how long it took to peel the pants off after the shoot.

The video, set in the darkened foyer of a Manhattan courthouse, appears to have employed the entire senior class of a Lower East Side high school. The percussive, dance-rich video succeeds in linking Shania with urban youth and rock—both the antithesis of traditional country music.

If Shania turned the corner onto Rock 'n' Roll Boulevard with "I'm Outta Here," then she parked her '55 Chevy right on the street with "You Win My Love." Steven Goldmann settles for a fairly literal translation of the song, with a racing car theme as the primary motif. Shania alternates between a dance sequence set against a billowing black checkered flag in the background and a goofy scene in which she plays bumper cars with four cute, college-age guys. In "You Win My Love," Shania, looking vaguely like Cindy Crawford with her faux beauty mark and straight hair, portrays a tough rock 'n' roll chick with class (accentuated by a leather-look plastic jacket and pants, leather gloves and a black bra under a white shirt). Her high-energy antics, including a few cartwheels, hint at the potential for an extremely physical live show. Like "I'm Outta Here," "You Win My Love" proves that Shania's authentic youthful exuberance does not have to be sacrificed in the name of traditional country music.

Steven Goldmann's fifth video with Shania, "No One Needs to Know," is one of his most effective, even though it is fairly sedate compared with the others. Most of the movement in this clip relates to the physical forces of nature—tornadoes and windstorms. The video opens with a casually dressed Shania rehearsing with her (fictional) band on the steps of an antebellum southern mansion. As the wind begins to pick up, the group moves indoors, where they continue playing in the drawing room of the house, amidst swinging chandeliers and a steadily building wind. In the final scene, Shania succeeds in slamming shut an unusually large front door that reveals a tornado bearing down on the house. The video is captivating and refreshing, following as it does a string of effective, but overproduced, minimovies. In the scene with the tornado outside the open door, you can almost imagine Shania thinking, This doesn't feel like Timmins anymore.

Besides the video released to promote the single "No One Needs to Know," another version was created using footage from the movie *Twister*, which featured the song on its sound track.

All three songs reached the number one spot on the *Billboard* Hot Country Singles chart, and the videos echoed that performance on CMT and TNN. But by late summer 1996, the CD was beginning to show signs of fatigue, even though album sales were still strong. The final two releases of the album, "Home Ain't Where His Heart Is (Anymore)" and a remixed version of "God Bless the Child," went to number 28 and 48, respectively, on the *Billboard* charts. The video for "God Bless the Child," however, was a big hit on TNN and CMT Canada, where it reached the number one spots.

There was a one-year gap between the release of the final single, "God Bless the Child," off *The Woman in Me*, and "Love Gets Me Every Time," the first single off Shania's third CD, *Come on Over*. Not surprisingly, Shania reinvented herself, visually and attitude-wise, in the intervening year. The first two videos from her new CD had virtually no stylistic or thematic link with any of her previous eleven video clips. This shift is indicative of Shania's chameleon-like visual persona, as well as her musical evolution as a singer and songwriter.

The long-anticipated debut of *Come on Over* proved one critical fact about Shania—she had not lost any of her appeal or popularity during her one-year hiatus. In fact, her first release, "Love Gets Me Every Time," took only six weeks to reach the number one spot on the *Billboard* Hot

Country Singles chart, where it stayed for five weeks. In video format, the song raced to number one on CMT Canada in record time.

"Love Gets Me Every Time," directed by Timothy Whyte of Automatic, is effective in its utter simplicity. Shania arrives backstage at a theater. She rifles through racks and racks of costumes and clothes, and tries on a lot of them. The camera follows her like a voyeur, never really letting the viewer see too much, but still offering an intimate glimpse inside Shania's dressing room. She shuffles around in a robe and a pair of oversized floppy slippers. She eats some boring-looking food. Every now and then, there are scenes of Shania at a photo shoot (which also appear on her CD liner notes). It's a charming, completely benign video. Its popularity is probably due to the fact that it portrays Shania playing herself for a change—not a cowgirl, foreign princess, model or race car driver. It's somehow refreshing to imagine that Shania might actually look like one of us when she is schlumping around in a robe.

Larry Jordan of Automatic directed the video clip for "Don't Be Stupid (You Know I Love You)." Picking up on the fiddle-rich song, the video portrays Shania and a Celtic dance troupe stomping through a series of Irish dances on a water-covered floor. The water splashes crazily, drenching Shania and the dancers. The video capitalizes on the international success of the "River Dance" phenomenon, but it also pays tribute to Shania's own Irish heritage (her mother was Irish, and her biological father is French-Irish). It could also be another sign that Mercury and PolyGram are positioning *Come on Over* for a major international distribution effort. "Don't Be Stupid," the video, quickly raced to the top spot on the CMT charts, although it was followed more slowly on the *Billboard* Hot Country Singles chart.

By early 1998, Shania was a veteran of over a dozen music videos, and the recipient of some of the music industry's most prestigious video awards, including a 1995 Canadian Country Music Award for Best Video ("Any Man of Mine"), the 1996 CMT Female Video Artist of the Year award, the 1996 Canadian Country Music Award for Best Video ("(If You're Not in It for Love) I'm Outta Here"), the 1996 CMT Europe Best Video Artist and Best Video of the Year awards ("Any Man of Mine") and a 1996 ABC Radio Networks Country Music Award for Female Video Artist of the Year for *The Woman in Me.* In addition, three of her videos made it to Canada's list of Top 12 Videos of 1996. On CMT USA, she had two videos in the top 5 and 4 in the top 100 in their annual fan-voted contest.

Shania's take on her video magic is that, much like an actress, she plays "characters" in her videos. Some of the characters just happen to be mildly provocative. In *New Country* magazine she is quoted as saying, "How far would I go? Well, I would never make sexual videos. It's not me. I'm uninhibited as an entertainer, but there's a line I'd draw. I'm into performing and having fun."

Her ever-changing video personas have also become her method of avoiding being typecast, which happens commonly in the music industry. Rather than be referred to as the singer with the hat or the black leather jacket, Shania makes a serious effort to defy categorization. As a result, the descriptions of Shania lean more toward adjectives— energetic, sexy and youthful.

When Twain was selected for CMT's February 1996

Showcase Artist, she said that videos had been a "big part" of her success in 1995. There is little doubt that they will continue to be an integral part of her career, and that her fans can expect ten pleasant video surprises from *Come on Over*.

## CHAPTER EIGHT

# SHANIA IN CYBERSPACE

cmiller

*Where can I find out where Shania was born? I want to go on a pilgrimage to her hometown next summer. Hey, maybe if enough people go we can have a party!*

mmgirl

*I am absolutely crazy about Come on Over. I heard that there's going to be at least ten singles off it. I'm going to bet my husband five bucks that every single makes it to the Top 10.*

marthaX12

*I heard that Shania isn't going to tour Canada. How can she turn her back on her own country? Is she an American citizen now? Doesn't she have any loyalty to us? So maybe I'll have to drive to Seattle to see her concert. Actually, that might be fun.*

samdamon
*Where can I get Shania's first CD in France? Some of the record stores in Paris have never heard of her!*

jjsimpson
*Hey, hunterman. Shania was born in Windsor on August 28, 1965. She moved when she was two years old to Timmins, Ontario.*

sixteen
*Please take note, "texasguy." This is not a LeAnn Rimes message board. If you feel the need to praise LeAnn and put down Shania here, you're definitely not wanted. LeAnn's biggest fans are eleven years old. At least Shania's fans are old enough to vote. Besides, LeAnn's CDs only sell a couple million each. That's how many copies Shania sold of WIM in the first month!!!*

biggestfan
*Hey, I just found out that Shania is going to launch her tour in Canada. That's only proper, since this IS her home country. Please please visit Edmonton, Shania! We need you up here.*

◆  ◆  ◆

It was simple being a music fan back in the old days, say before 1995. If you liked a singer, you bought her album, tuned into the radio stations that played her music and then every couple of years bought tickets to see her live in concert when her tour visited the nearest big city.

If you were a particularly avid fan, you might watch her music videos on a cable video channel, or check the TV listings to see if she was performing that week on *Saturday Night Live* or *The Tonight Show with Jay Leno*.

Being the fan of an entertainer used to be a private experience. If you discussed your admiration at all, it was with a friend or family member, not a stranger on the other side of the world.

Then along came the World Wide Web. Suddenly, it became possible to take a simple case of fan adulation and turn it into an international networking experience. It doesn't matter who you are a fan of—Yogi Bear, Shania Twain or Harrison Ford. There are home pages and tributes to virtually every entertainer in existence, and many of them offer a chat line or E-mail access to people who share your affection for the entertainer.

Shania Twain is no exception. In fact, she exploded on the country music scene on a virtual parallel course with the Web. It's never been necessary to passively wait for news on Shania—by simply typing in her name on any of the search engines on the Internet, you are rewarded with thousands of potential sites to visit. Since Shania's name is unique, most sites that you find when you do a name search on the Internet actually refer to "the" Shania Twain. On Alta Vista, for example, you will find more than 2,000 documents dedicated completely or partly to Shania; Info Seek connects to 3,000 sites; and on Hot Bot, more than 9,300 sites show a direct reference to Shania. The documents, however, vary widely in how much data they include on her, from elaborate home pages devoted solely to Shania, to radio stations or magazines that have articles or references to her in their database, to official sites set up by her record label, to brief mentions in someone's tribute page to country music.

There are about a dozen major tribute pages on the Internet that are completely dedicated to Shania. Few, if any, of the people who maintain these sites have ever had direct contact with Shania, her record label or her management company (with the exception of official fan club home pages). The superfan who creates these time-consuming tribute pages does so as a result of pure admiration for Shania, not for financial gain. The hosts of these pages rely on newspaper and magazine articles, television interviews and unofficial "tips" from fans for their content. Some of the sites boast extensive photo galleries of images scanned from CDs, magazine articles and amateur snapshots.

The accuracy in reporting, not surprisingly, is inconsistent. Some sites have inaccurate information. One popular web site, for instance, "Talon's Page," which is part of "The Definitive Shania Twain Pages," posts a biography that claims Shania was raised by adoptive parents (she was raised by her natural mother and adoptive father), sang in nightclubs at the age of five (she was eight), raised one brother alone (she raised her two teenaged brothers and a sister after her parents died) and worked for her father's "afforestation" business where she would go into the forest for months and only come out every two weeks for groceries (most of the crew members of the *re*forestation company, including Shania, returned to Timmins and other towns on weekends). Even her own label, Mercury Nashville, contributes to inaccuracy in web journalism. Shania's biography at that site incorrectly claims her parents were killed when she was twenty-one (an error that appears in about 75 percent of all articles on Shania). In fact, Shania's parents' accident took place on November 1, 1987. Shania had turned twenty-two a few months earlier, on August 28, 1987.

The Internet is a remarkable source of current media and archival material on Shania. Several magazines and newspaper sites store articles on her, including *Billboard, USA Today, Entertainment Weekly, People,* and *Country Music Weekly.* Some publications, like *USA Today,* charge a small fee to users who want to download articles. One of the best sources of media coverage on Shania is Canada's "Canoe" media site, which features dozens of full-text articles that have appeared in Canadian newspapers and magazines. Some of the private tribute pages, such as Liz's "Shania Filez," include articles and reviews from a variety of ources that date back to 1995.

Liz's "Shania Filez" (http://www.geocities.com/Hollywood/Hills/1130/index.html) is arguably the best Shania tribute page on the Internet. The site features sparse but elegant graphics, current reporting and the authoritative air of an "official" site. The Shania Filez is designed and maintained by "Liz," a sixteen-year-old high school student from the Toronto area who writes poetry in her spare time and hangs out at the Second Cup coffee shop with her friends.

Besides Shania, her musical tastes run to Mariah Carey, the Goo Goo Dolls, Moist, Real McCoy, Celine Dion and Toni Braxton.

The "Shania Filez" is frequently the most accurate and up-to-date source of news on Shania. News briefs are updated weekly (except maybe during exams at Liz's high school) and are dated to indicate when they were posted. Liz's postings are articulate and friendly, often with witty asides and observations.

Steve Sque of England was one of the first fans to launch a Shania Twain home page (it operated from 1996 to 1998). His "Shania Twain Superland" site was overflowing with monumental and trite information about the country singer. Presented in an upbeat, bright style with flashing icons and moving messages, "Superland" was an elaborate, extensive tribute. The twenty-one-item menu offered visitors a choice of guitar transcripts to some of Shania's songs, a message forum, news articles, a chat line, a Shania quiz, a letter from Shania to her fans and the "complete ultimate" picture gallery. The site had the unmistaken feeling of being the brainchild of a guy with a serious, but innocent, crush on Shania.

Steve was planning his own home page tribute to Shania when he came across an existing Shania site on the net, maintained by another Brit, Gordon Lee. Steve was surprised to find out that he wasn't the "only English guy who'd heard of her." Gordon responded to Steve's E-mail and informed him that he was already sharing resources with Dan (aka Talon), a Shania fan in Canada. The three chatted (cyberously) and decided to collaborate on a linked group of web sites that they called "The Definitive Shania Twain Pages."

Steve, who has never seen Shania live, started his page as a tribute to her work and as a resource for her fans. One of the primary, and most popular, features on Steve's page was the chat room and the message forum, both of which offered fans the chance to post their opinions and questions about Shania. The message forum (though occasionally misused by anonymous depraved individuals who hijacked the forum to post inappropriate messages) was mainly used by fervent Shania fans to praise her albums and ask when she'd be performing live in their area. Occasionally a message would generate a lively discussion on some aspect of Shania's career (debates on the merits of one album over another were common), with comments being posted over a period of a few days. The chat room offered almost real-time conversations about Shania, or on any other subject dear to the hearts of Shania fans. The chat room was frequented by the type of visitors you might find at a high school junior prom. The cyber conversations posted at this site were often about topics other than Shania and her music.

Steve strived to keep his site virtually maintenance-free, with the Chat Room and Message Forum driven by fans' postings, and the other menu items connected to permanent archives or links to other Shania sites on the Web.

The fact that over a quarter of a million people visited the site since it was established in 1996 is a source of amazement for Steve's parents and friends. Many visitors were hard-core fans who popped in every week or so for an update, or to leave an opinion on the Message Forum.

Steve was never surprised or shocked at what he found posted on the Message Forum at his web site, but the following are some of the ones he considers the most interesting:

"We were neighbors of Shania's back in 1983. This is before her famous days (she was a tree planter then). We have stayed friends with her sister Jill. I babysat her little brothers a few times while her mom went to bingo. She comes from a nice Northern Ontario type family. Glad you made it big Shania. Don't forget your roots."

"I come to the Shania Twain web site only to see if there are any new pictures of Shania in swimwear or anything else that reveals her boobies. Anyone who worships Shania Twain for her musical talent is as much of an ignorant hick as your cousins tell you."

"WOW, this is neat!!!! I used to HATE country music until I heard Shania Twain's song 'Any Man of Mine.' I luv that song."

"I'm sure that anyone HERE won't agree with me, but Shania's career is basically built on lies. No one should use the story of a parent's death to win people over. And as for her claim of Indian ancestry . . . that was just plain disrespectful. It is a good thing she looks the way she does because if she had to do it on singing ability . . . this page wouldn't exist. One thing left to say. . . . Milli Vanilli."

"Hi, I'd just like to say that I think Shania has the most beautiful voice and every time I listen to her CD it makes me feel wonderful. I live in Brisbane, Australia, and hope that Shania tours Australia soon. If you see this Shania, I hope you know how special a person you are."

"Shania has tried to compromise between the two styles (rock and country) with little success. Shania, make up your mind on what your preference is! If you want to do country rock go and listen to Stevie Nicks' 'Bella Donna' for some inspiration. PS: To all those who write vulgar/ crude comments to this forum go to the XXX pages to get your cheap thrills. Don't bore us with your crap!!!"

"Zeke, you are absolutely right. The WIM album is far superior to the first album because as you said Shania could not contribute as much of her talent as she could on the WIM. She was 'molded' by the Nashville song writers and told what people wanted to hear. This resulted in a situation which sets a great artist apart from everyone else. It is much easier to go and get a song from a writer than it is to write a song from your heart. Shania wrote songs from her heart, soul and life experiences on the WIM album and this is why it is a superior production. I must also add here that one of my favorite songs from her first album is 'God Ain't Gonna Getcha for That' which not surprisingly is the only one of Shania's own songs that was included on this album."

"Shania Twain is an undeniably, incredibly beautiful woman. What some people tend to forget is her wonderful singing talent. Her music lifts me up and always puts a smile on my face. She's awesome, in every way possible. Her husband is a lucky man."

Steve is sometimes surprised by reports of negative press that Shania has received in Canada and the United

States about her Aboriginal ancestry and how she handled the firing of manager Mary Bailey. He claims that the British press simply doesn't cover that aspect of her career, and that he doesn't listen to that type of media coverage anyway. His primary goal was to maintain a tribute to Shania's work, and give her fans a fun place to go to learn more about her.

Although Steve maintained his Shania Twain home page with a high level of sophistication and integrity, some of the other special-interest sections on his home pages were considerably more risqué than his Shania Twain site.

Talon (aka Dan) met Steve through Gordon Lee. He was searching for Shania sites at www.yahoo.com and found Gordon's page. After he sent a note complimenting him on the site, they started corresponding regularly by E-mail. Steve and Gordon invited Talon (www.mnsi.net/~talon/shania.htm) to join their coalition of pages called "The Definitive Shania Twain Pages." Though they have never met, other than in cyberspace, they are all good friends.

Operating out of Windsor, Ontario (ironically, the city where Shania was born), Talon is the only one of the "three amigos" who has seen Shania perform live. He attended the Fan Appreciation Day at the Canadian National Exhibition (CNE) in Toronto on August 17, 1996, when Shania met several thousand fans and performed one song.

Talon started a tribute page partly because he had access to free web space, and because he considers himself a big fan of hers. When he started out in 1996, there were few sites on Shania that offered anything more than pictures and a biography. Talon wanted to produce a quality page that had everything a Shania fan could want, something he feels "The Definitive Shania Twain Pages" come close to achieving.

Unlike Steve, who tried to keep his site fairly low-maintenance, Talon spends about five hours a week updating and monitoring the site (which he visits almost every day).

The number of visitors to Talon's site varies, depending on if Shania has just released a new album or single, but he generally gets about a hundred visitors a day. Most people who maintain tribute pages to celebrities are amazed at how many people think that *they* are the celebrity. Messages are often sent by E-mail to "Shania," and can sometimes be quite sincere and friendly. To Steve, Gordon and Talon's knowledge, Shania has never visited their tributes to her on the Internet.

In fact, none of the three sites have ever had official contact with Shania, her management company or Mercury Nashville, her record label. Sometimes they get information from friends of friends of friends who are connected to Shania in some way. There's no doubt that an actual face-to-face meeting with Shania would be a thrill of a lifetime for Steve, Gordon and Dan.

Talon has learned to tolerate negative press about Shania, but accepts the fact that much of it is based on rumors or arises out of jealousy. He's confident that most of her fans support her, and some are quite vocal on the Message Forum about dispelling the negative comments. Like many of the fans who visit "The Definitive Shania

Twain Pages," Talon is motivated by complete admiration for Shania.

The most opinionated and radical of the Shania pages is her "official" fan club site (http://www.shania.com). Known affectionately to fans as Shania-dot-com, the site is managed by a protective web master known as Trace, who is Shania's self-appointed cyber security guard and head cheerleader. It sports more exclamation marks per hundred words than any other site on the Web. In Internet jargon, posting in capital letters is the equivalent of shouting. If this is the case, then Trace must have an extremely hoarse voice. The entire site is presented in a frantic mode, with every single news item an earth-shattering occurrence, and every perceived error or slight by Shania's label or a video channel a national crisis. It's an addictive site, mainly because the text is so emotionally charged and takes itself so seriously.

Trace is frequently critical of the way that Mercury Nashville and PolyGram have handled the sales and marketing of Shania's three albums. (His persistent claim of Mercury Nashville's lack of support is hard to justify, considering that *The Woman in Me* sold over nine million units in the United States, and three million in Canada and other countries, which couldn't have occurred without a high degree of label championing.) The following are some excerpts of Trace's reporting style at Shania-dot-com:

"Shania's "WIM" is RIAA certified for U.S. sales of over 9 million albums . . . obliterating EVERY previous record— THE FASTEST (by years)/BEST SELLING ALBUM (by over 3 million) by a female country artist EVER!! (even more amazing with NO promotional media campaign of any kind on TV or in print, due to her label's continuing and inexcusable lack of support) . . ."

Trace doesn't give PolyGram any more credit for its international distribution efforts: ". . . . hopefully, if her parent company PolyGram would finally start to do its job, 'WIM' will finally start to become more 'globally' available and its sales skyrocket worldwide."

Shania-dot-com is congested with trivia, news, facts, rumors, performance schedules and chart information, with no apparent indexing plan to offer readers more digestible-size news bits.

When *Country Music Weekly* covered the story about Shania's biological father, Trace put the publication on his hit list and began referring to it as a "rag." It didn't seem to matter that the magazine has featured Shania on numerous covers and has given her some of her most extensive and consistently positive media since the mid-1990s.

Shania-dot-com, regardless of its editorial policy, is a proactive Shania support machine. It urges fans to vote for her video on CMT and on fan-voted awards programs, and to call country stations to request her songs. If Trace comes across as an overbearing one-man cheering squad, it's tempered by his seemingly genuine devotion to Shania. The site is also equipped to sell Shania's CDs, posters and other merchandise.

The Australian Shania Twain Fanclub (http://www.fan.net.au/~ronnie/) is operated by Video Entertainment International. In early 1998, this site joined up with the Shania Twain Mailing List Supersite (Shania-dot-com) to offer the Shania Twain International On-Line Fan Club.

Proving that Shania Twain is alive and well in the southern hemisphere, the site offers an Australian spin on Shania news, with references to radio stations and retailers in that part of the world. Most information, however, is channeled from American and Canadian Shania tribute pages and the North American media. New visitors might be confused by the months of old news, some of it undated, that you must scroll through before you get to the most recent Shania newsletters. Organizing news with the newest at the end is mainly a design weakness, and you do eventually reach the current newsletters. Deleting the ancient history would make the site more lively and fresh, especially after reading endless announcements of the "soon-to-be-released" CD, *Come on Over*.

The site is chatty, and frequently uses a polite and reverent approach, a sharp contrast to Trace's style at Shania-dot-com. For example, the site starts out with such courteous requests as, "Please remember to vote for Shania at Blockbuster sites," and "Thanks for your help and support." Ronnie, the CEO and master of the site, rarely "shouts" the news, except when he inserts excerpts from Trace's page. Cyber friendships and collaborations seem to be the norm in the world of celebrity tribute pages on the Web.

The Australian site is one of the few pages that pays tribute to people closely associated with Shania, such as her ex-guitarists (from her 1995–96 band) Dan Schafer and David Malachowski.

A visit to Daniel's Shania Twain home page (http://www.geocities.com/Nashville/7321/) proves that she is one of the most photographed singers in North America.

The site features over 230 scanned images, mainly from published sources and her CDs. Los Angeles–based Daniel, like most urban high school students, didn't even listen to country until he saw Shania on the *Billboard* Music Awards in 1995. He was so impressed by her voice that he decided to dedicate a tribute page to her. His list of favorite bands includes AC/DC and Led Zeppelin (ironically, both produced by Mutt Lange in the 1980s) and country artists Garth Brooks and Alan Jackson.

Daniel's site is lean and to the point, and the news is generally current (most of it culled from Trace's site, which he acknowledges). The design of the site—yellow text superimposed over a multiple image of Shania—makes it extremely difficult to read on the computer screen. The amazing collection of photographs, however, is really the primary attraction at this site.

Tribute pages produced by superfans are not the only place to learn about Shania's latest escapades and life history. There are numerous media resource centers and music organizations that serve as excellent guides.

One of the best is Canada's "Canoe" (http://www.canoe.ca/Jam/home.html), a media center that links the archives of a number of the country's magazines and newspapers under one "roof." Visitors who find their way into the search room are rewarded with dozens of current and past full-text articles on Shania that have appeared in Canadian publications.

The three North American country music channels available on cable TV—Country Music Television Canada, Country Music Television USA and The Nashville Network—all have their own web sites where you can access broadcast schedules, country news briefs and related country music information.

CMT Canada (http://www.canoe.ca/CMT/home2.html) never lets you forget that Canada is Shania's home and native land. The Daily Top 12 videos, which are voted on by fans electronically, frequently feature Shania in the top spot. Basically, if she has a current video in rotation, her loyal fans up north will keep the clip in the Top 5 for months. When *Come on Over* debuted in late 1997, the first two releases, "Love Gets Me Every Time" and "Don't Be Stupid," virtually planted themselves in the one-two spots for several weeks.

One of CMT Canada's best features is the daily video airplay schedule. This service gives a minute-by-minute timetable of the videos that are airing on the station that day. CMT Country Music Beat is also an excellent offering, and a significant amount of the late-breaking Shania news found on the Web's tribute pages first appeared on this CMT feature.

CMT USA (http://www.country.com/cmt/cmt-f.html) is not as interactive or up to the minute as its northern counterpart, but it is a valuable site to bookmark. Unlike Canada, where Shania rules, CMT USA plays her videos extensively, but not obsessively. The first two clips from *Come on Over* did not make it to the channel's 1997 Top 20 list, while in Canada they both were among the Top 20 videos of the year.

CMT USA also provides links to CMT channels in Europe, Latin America and the Pacific Rim. A scan of the top videos on these global outlets shows that while Shania is a favorite, her videos do not get heavy rotation until a few months after they peak in North America.

TNN USA (http://www.country.com/tnn/tnn-f.html) is a more typical specialty channel than CMT. TNN's schedule is more of a "country lifestyle" channel—it features diverse programming, including country video clips, talk shows, country history programs, live concerts and outdoor and sports shows. Shania's first video off *The Woman in Me*, "Whose Bed Have Your Boots Been Under?", did not get picked up by TNN, but it aired her subsequent videos, many of which made it to TNN's number one spot. This specialty channel leans more toward "traditional country" music and lifestyles, while CMT is more of a "New Country" channel, which more clearly caters to Shania's brand of music.

The only true "official" Shania site on the Web is at the address of her label, Mercury Nashville (http://www.mecurynashville.com). Even though *Come on Over* was released under the Mercury label (the Nashville conspicuously absent), this Music City label is where you'll find the corporation's primary site on Shania. The most recent addition is a series of photos from her latest video, radio interviews and music clips, an up-to-date biography (the previous version wasn't changed for close to three years) and information on her CD releases.

Shania fans who want to track her sales and radio airplay can go to two respected music industry charting organizations—the *Gavin Report* and *Billboard* magazine.

Gavin (http://www.gavin.com) tracks airplay on 200 country radio stations, with weekly updates on Thursday. The charts are based on a rating formula that takes total spins and radio station adds into consideration when determining the strength of a single.

*Billboard*'s home page (http://www.billboard.com) offers limited access to its charts. The magazine is obviously reluctant to offer full access to its lists on the Web, since thousands of music industry companies and individuals pay premium rates to receive them in printed and electronic formats every week. It is still possible to get a limited view of its Top 200 Albums, Top Country Albums and Hot Country Singles, however. *Billboard*'s criteria for ratings on its charts is based on sales, with the exception being its singles charts, which are based on radio airplay. *USA Today* (http://www.usatoday.com) posts a summarized version of the *Billboard* charts at its web site every week. The national newspaper has covered Shania news on many occasions over the past five years, and you can download articles for $1 each at this site.

The only drawback to the World Wide Web is that it is inaccessible to millions of people who don't have computers, modems and Internet accounts. Public libraries, cyber cafes, the office and schools are alternatives to being left out in the cold. Shania World is never more than a minute away if you're connected to the World Wide Web.

The question remaining is whether Shania cruises the Internet reading her fan mail and checking out the country music charts. Steve Sque says he has never come across an apparition on the Web that might be Shania. If she is secretly visiting her fan-driven tribute sites on the Web, she's probably touched by the level of dedication and support these mega-fans are giving her. While the Web may not be the sole reason she sold thirteen million copies of *The Woman in Me* (something Trace would like to have us believe), it certainly didn't hurt.

Maybe someday Shania will wander into "The Definitive Shania Twain Pages" or Shania-dot-com and leave a quick note of thanks to those devoted fans who spend countless hours building their shrines to her on the World Wide Web.

CHAPTER NINE

# FANS: LOYALTY AND PATIENCE

Dear Shania,

I don't know if you ever get these letters that fans send you, but I thought I'd you send one anyway. Who knows, maybe you read them on the tour bus when you're on your way to the next concert. I just hope that your record label forwards this letter to you.

I've never actually written to a celebrity before. Although I don't really think of you as a celebrity. You're more like someone I might have gone to high school with who made it big. You would have been a freshman when I was a senior. In fact, there was a girl in my school who was a lot like you must have been. Really pretty and talented too. She sang the national anthem at all the ball games, and she had her own country band. I don't know what happened to her. I think she moved to Nashville right out of high school.

Well, the reason I'm writing to you is because of something

*that happened recently between my daughter and me. It had to do with your music, so I thought it might be of interest to you.*

*Vanessa, my daughter, is fourteen going on twenty-five. You know the phase. Short skirts, black eyeliner, really snide remarks when anyone asks her what she's up to. She used to be warm and sweet. We got along super until she hit thirteen. I think what happened is that she discovered some really dark, negative music through some friends of hers. No, you can't really call it music. It sounds like a couple cats stuck in the clothes dryer. You know, thump thump thump, yeowww. It had to do with all sorts of negative things, like people having no hope, and the world not being worth saving, etc. etc. I listened to a few of her tapes, but they were so depressing that I just had to throw them out in the trash. Which made Vanessa go ballistic.*

*She didn't talk to me for days, so I finally decided to go out and buy her some new tapes, to replace the ones I'd tossed out. I thought to myself . . . should I buy the same depressing tapes for her? Well, I didn't. Instead, I bought her tapes by two terrific women singers—Jann Arden and Shania Twain. When I gave her the tapes I said I couldn't sit back and let her miss out on all the amazing, wonderful music that was available. She didn't say a thing.*

*A couple days later she came home after school in almost a pleasant mood. She said, Thanks for the tapes, Mom. She admitted that she didn't even like the other ones, but that everyone in her group was listening to them and she felt like she had to fit in, so she listened too. Well, she liked Jann Arden, even her song "Good Mother" (so maybe I slipped that song in for a reason). She REALLY loves your music. Especially "Man! I Feel Like a Woman!", which she wants her girlfriends to adopt as their Fri-*

*day night going out song, and "Whatever You Do! Don't!"*
*which worries me because I didn't even think she NOTICED*
*boys yet.*

*Anyway, if you make it to Phoenix on your tour, I'm going*
*to buy tickets for Vanessa and her friend Toby and me. Of course*
*they'll probably make me sit up in the top row or something, or*
*pretend I don't know them. Whatever. It's just good to know that*
*there's something that Vanessa and I have in common now—we*
*both love your music.*

*Yours truly,*
*Carmen D.*
*Phoenix, Arizona*

*P.S. When you finally have children, feel free to write to*
*me for tips! I've also got a nine-year-old daughter, Amanda,*
*who still thinks I'm cool.*

◆　　◆　　◆

Country music is about getting close to the people, Doug
Chappel, the president of PolyGram USA, once said. To
most country recording artists, getting "close to the people" translates into hitting the road in a custom tour bus
(complete with a media system and a minibar) and two 16-
wheelers full of sound, light and musical equipment for a
grueling 200-city North American concert tour. Each stop
means a packed schedule of record store autograph sessions, drop-ins at music stores, interviews at the local country radio station and meeting a whole slew of local people
backstage after the concert. Being everywhere, though,
doesn't necessarily mean connecting with people. There are

many artists who don't have the patience or desire to reach their fans on a person-to-person level. They view their stardom as a business, and they may go through all the motions of being friendly and down-home, but in reality they are just doing their job.

Shania's decision not to follow the obligatory touring route to support her second release, *The Woman in Me,* perplexed and/or annoyed many people in the country music industry. Some interpreted her decision not to tour as an excuse for lacking the talent to carry a live show, while others considered it the sign of a recording artist out of touch with her audience. To some, not touring was the equivalent of simply not caring about one's fans.

Shania's hiatus from touring lasted five years—from spring 1993 (the end of her fifteen-city "Triple Play" tour with John Brannen and Toby Keith) until spring 1998 (the start of her world tour to support *Come on Over*). Though she failed to hit the concert trail during that time, Shania did not forget about the importance of "getting close to the people." She simply did it her way. This meant attending a number of Fan Appreciation events at malls and outdoor fairs in the United States and Canada, in 1995 and 1996, to support *The Woman in Me,* and in the fall of 1997 to help launch *Come on Over.* Shania did not treat these events like a perfunctory duty. She put her heart and soul into them— signing thousands of autographs, premiering her videos, talking to fans, picking up babies, singing her songs a cappella (she did not bring her band) and holding question-and-answer sessions with fans.

Shania has proven to be a celebrity who doesn't erect superficial barriers between herself and her fans at these types of public events. She manages to communicate on a genuinely warm level, making it feel like there's nowhere else on earth that she'd rather be than in a crowded suburban shopping mall, meeting and greeting her devoted fans.

That doesn't mean that Shania is not aware of the realities of being a celebrity in America. She is almost always accompanied by Tim, her tan German shepherd companion, and when she is in large crowds, by a few security guards.

Shania's Fan Appreciation tours in 1996 and 1997 actually gave her devotees a vastly different experience than they would have had if she had gone on a concert tour. First of all, the Fan Appreciation events are free. In order to meet her, one need only live near one of the cities or towns where she makes her royal visits.

But catching a glimpse of the Canadian diva may require sacrifices. It might mean missing a day at work or school, driving a long way to a mall or fairground, searching frantically for a parking spot within a country mile of the venue, standing in a long line in the hopes of getting picked for an autograph, sizzling under an afternoon sun in an outdoor park, experiencing the throat-tightening sensation of being in the midst of a crowd of 20,000 who are all singing "Even when I'm ugly, he still better love me," in loud, out-of-tune voices and realizing that the rest room line is forty people long. The rewards, though, are worth it—a roughly 10 percent chance of getting picked to receive Shania's autograph, watching sneak previews of her latest video, singing one or two of her hits with her and 20,000 other people and, with any luck, landing a few seconds of conversation with Shania, after which you might take home a piece of music history in the form of an autograph.

Malls and parks may satisfy some fans' appetites, but for the hard-core country fan, Fan Fair in Nashville is the ultimate thrill. The gathering takes place every June at the Tennessee Fair Grounds in Nashville. Sponsored by the Country Music Association, fans snap up the 24,000 tickets weeks before the event. The attraction is that you have access to close to 400 of country music's biggest and newest recording artists making nonstop appearances onstage, in autograph booths, at special parties for fans and on the baseball field. It's a country music fan's nirvana.

The only place on earth that a fan could have seen Shania singing more than one song in a row with a band at a public event was at Fan Fairs 1993, 1994, 1995 or 1996 (she canceled her attendance at the 1997 event because she was in the studio recording her third album, *Come on Over*). Shania had her own signing booth in 1996, as well as a special party for Shania Twain Fan Club members who had purchased tickets in advance.

In August 1995, not long after *The Woman in Me* became the number one country album in Canada and the United States, Shania cohosted a special daylong Fan Fest at Canada's Wonderland Amusement Park, north of Toronto. Mercury made the surprise announcement that her album had reached double platinum (200,000) in Canada and a couple of million in the United States. She sang "Any Man of Mine" that day, accompanied by 5,000 of her newest fans.

Shortly after the event at Wonderland, Shania and her then manager, Mary Bailey, made the decision not to tour to support her hit album. That winter, Shania began making highly publicized appearances at Fan Appreciation Days. Her first took place at the Mall of the Americas in

Bloomington, Minnesota, in February 1996. A crowd estimated at 20,000 people—the mall's second largest attendance ever, other than its opening day—showed up. Shania thrilled the crowd when she got up on the massive speakers and danced and sang along with videos of her that were being shown on large screens. The following month, Shania enthralled a crowd estimated to be 20,000 strong outside Planet Hollywood in Dallas.

Perhaps one of the most memorable days in Shania's life came on August 15, 1996, when her hometown of Timmins, Ontario, honored her with the keys to the city. A jam-packed day had been planned to demonstrate Timmins's pride in her, and to attract some good publicity for the town itself.

The day started out drearily overcast. Shania's spirits, however, were far from being dampened, even as a steady rain fell throughout the day. A Shania Day planning committee, made up of prominent local leaders, had a full day of activities planned for Shania, starting with the presentation of the keys to the city by the mayor. Shania, clearly touched by the outpouring of devotion and love from her former neighbors, cracked that the rain wasn't a problem, because they were northerners and weren't made of sugar. As she looked into the audience that day, she saw the faces of people she had grown up with—her neighbors, classmates, bank tellers, grocery store clerks, gas station attendants, city council members, teachers and family members. It was perhaps the ultimate tribute that fans could bestow upon one of their own. Shania was visibly moved, and the tears welled up in her eyes many times that day.

The official delegation, followed by thousands of well-wishers, joined Shania at a public park, where a guitar-shaped flower garden was dedicated to her. Later, a portion of Highway 101, which runs through Timmins, was named "Shania Twain Way."

The evening was devoted to a special fund-raiser for local youth and arts organizations. The $100-a-plate dinner and performance by the Timmins Symphony was sold out. Near the end of the evening, the Timmins Symphony performed the "Shania Waltz," which had been commissioned by the city. The moment was especially poignant for Shania, whose family was in the audience, including her brothers and sisters, aunts and grandmother. The two people in Shania's life who were sadly missing that night were her parents, Sharon and Jerry. Had they not lost their lives in the accident, they would undoubtedly have been Shania's biggest fans.

Shania barely had time to recover from her emotional visit to Timmins when she hosted a Fan Appreciation Day at the Canadian National Exhibition (CNE) in Toronto on August 17, 1996. An estimated 10,000 people attended the event, some arriving before dawn in the hopes of getting one of the 500 wristbands that would guarantee a moment of Shania's attention and an autograph.

The event kicked off with a live concert by Canadian country artist Duane Steele. The young singer-songwriter from Hines Creek, Alberta, performed many of his songs from his debut album, *P.O. Box 423*. Ironically, Duane had arrived in Nashville shortly after Shania in the early 1990s, and had landed a songwriting contract with the prestigious publishing company Warner/Chappell. Though only in his early twenties, Duane has penned more than a hundred songs, including his own hits, "The Trouble with Love," "Anita Got Married" and "Two Names on an Overpass," a duet that he recorded with Lisa Brokop. After Duane's set, the stagehands began to prepare for Shania's arrival, while her videos played on a large screen behind the stage.

Shania stepped out onstage to a roaring welcome. A few presentations were made, including the two 1996 Junos for Best Country Music Vocalist and Entertainer of the Year that she had won earlier that year, but had not picked up due to a sudden case of the flu that had forced her to cancel her performance on the televised awards show. She was also presented with plaques for diamond sales in Canada of one million albums.

After listening to the standard acceptance speeches, the fans began to chant for what they had come for—some of Shania's music. Shania responded to their chant with an amused, "What exactly would you like me to sing without music?" Then she sang "No One Needs to Know," a cappella. Although she was supposed to leave immediately to catch a plane to Washington, D.C. (she was singing for the Clintons at the Ford Center the next day), she found time to stay a little longer to answer questions from the audience and to sign more autographs.

During the question-and-answer period, a young girl told her that it was her birthday, and she also offered Shania good wishes for her upcoming thirty-first birthday on August 28. Shania sang the child an endearing version of "Happy Birthday to You."

More than a year later, Shania was back with a new album, *Come on Over*, and many of her fans were still eager to hear her music and to see her live. She returned to the

Mall of the Americas in Bloomington, Minnesota, on November 4, 1997, where 20,000 people turned out to welcome Shania back. The lines had started forming at 6:30 A.M. that morning, and mall security had divided the crowd into two sections in different parts of the mall, to avoid a possibly dangerous surge of people when Shania arrived. Shania had repeated her wildly successful first visit to the mall. This time she was premiering her new video "Don't Be Stupid (You Know I Love You)," and in nearby record shops, her new CD *Come on Over* was well-stocked and prominently displayed on the shelves.

On November 9, 1997, Canada got a little of its own Shania-fever. This time, close to 27,000 fans jammed into a Fan Appreciation session at Southcentre Mall in Calgary, Alberta. Few seemed to care that Santa Claus, who was scheduled to set up shop at the mall that day to launch the Christmas season, had been bumped to the following day in order to allow Shania to use the "North Pole" area for her Fan Appreciation event. It isn't surprising that Shania's Calgary appearance attracted record crowds. The city is often called "Nashville North," because 40 percent of Canada's country albums are sold in the Calgary area.

Despite the huge crowds, Shania ventured into the midst of them several times during the afternoon, often to get to a fan in a wheelchair. She signed thousands of autographs on guitars, clothing, CD jackets, posters, cowboy hats and anything else available. In a replay of her Mall of the Americas performance, Shania showed videos, sang a few songs a cappella and climbed on top of massive speakers so that the fans in the back could see her. Dressed in black pants, a short belly button–revealing top and a light blue jacket, she did not disappoint even her youngest fans. She picked up babies so their parents could take photos, and she hugged young children who brought her gifts. Her adoring fans left her an enormous pile of flowers and gifts that included a handmade stick building with a sign that said, "Shania's Barn."

Shania's Fan Appreciation Days have been a message to her millions of fans that she cares about them and appreciates their support. Though the appearances have not reached many more than 100,000 people over two years, the news of the events has reached millions more. The impressive size of the crowds that attend these fan fests contribute to Shania's public image as a celebrity with mass appeal who has the heart to meet her fans one person at a time. It's possible that she will not be able to duplicate this type of intimate contact with her fans on her international concert tour, except perhaps on a much smaller scale. The time and energy demands of the tour will mean that Shania's fans will have to be content with seeing her onstage with her band, not hanging out with a couple thousand of her closest fans at the mall on a Saturday afternoon.

In the early days of Shania's recording career, she might not have been able to attract 20,000 fans at the biggest mall in America, but if one or two of them wanted to know more about her, they could contact either her Timmins or Nashville fan clubs.

Shania's "official" fan club has been managed and operated by a few close friends for several years—Helene Bolduc, the mother of her former fiancé, Paul Bolduc; and Cynthia Hagen, a close friend from high school. The fan club, which has an informal relationship with members of

Shania's staff, has played an important role in serving Shania's hard-core fans with accurate, authoritative information and news, as well as managing a constant flow of fan mail. The club's greatest disadvantage is that it has developed completely without access to Internet communications, such as a home page or E-mail.

The transition from printed material sent via "snail mail" to a World Wide Web–based electronic fan club is scheduled for 1998. Fans will still have to join the club, for a nominal fee, to have access to the postings and to receive club perks such as a 10 percent discount on merchandise, a photograph and a membership card.

Leading the charge to bring the fan club up to today's electronic standards are Trace at Shania-dot-com and Ronnie at Video International Network, the Australian Shania tribute page site.

Is there a "typical" Shania fan? According to an unscientific survey of radio programmers and web sites and a scan of audiences at some of her Fan Appreciation Days, the answer is no. Shania seems to attract men and women fans in almost equal proportions. Although women buy more albums than men, her sex appeal has definitely motivated men to join the legions of women who are snapping up copies of her tapes and CDs at a record-breaking pace. But Shania-mania attracts people of all ages, sexes and cultures. People are simply attracted to Shania, whether it's due to her poignant childhood, clever songs, addictive videos or a sensual quality that appeals to men and women alike.

Shania is someone who will give a guy a friendly smile, a baby a cuddle, a child a kind word, a woman a knowing smile and a person with a learning disability all the time in the world. Shania will never be short of fans, because she is someone who not only understands that "country music is about getting close to the people," but is willing to hold on to that conviction regardless of how big a celebrity she becomes.

## CHAPTER TEN

# THE ROAD AHEAD

*The small sign on the door of the nightclub in this seaside town says, "Closed for private event." The steady stream of limousines that have been arriving at the club's side door all evening and the burly, tuxedoed bouncers hint at the exclusive audience that has gathered inside.*

*It is New Year's Eve, 1999. In every part of the world, enthusiastic revelers are celebrating the transition into the twenty-first century. Inside this dark-paneled club there are no more than 150 people in the audience, all of them connected to Shania in one way or another. Her closest friends, family (even the elusive Mutt), managers, music critics, radio and video program directors and record label executives fill the cabaret-style tables. There are also ten people in the audience who count themselves among her luckiest fans. They have traveled from every corner of the world as winners in the "Shania 2000" contest sponsored by*

CMT's five stations in the United States, Canada, Europe, Latin America and the Pacific Rim.

Massive bouquets of flowers imported from Brazil, an elegant seafood feast and free-flowing French champagne fill the room. Purple and blue balloons, suspended in a huge net hooked up to the ceiling, wait patiently for the freedom that awaits them at the stroke of midnight. Throughout the room, camera crews from HBO and CMT have staked out their camera locations. Operators with handheld cameras are roaming conspicuously amongst the audience. It's hard not to be somewhat nervous, knowing that Shania's concert will be beamed instantly to seventy-nine countries via satellite transmission, with a potential world audience of half a billion people. Everyone in the club seems to be engaged in animated conversations as they try to pretend that there are no cameras in the room.

At eleven o'clock, the emcee for the evening, veteran journalist Dave Marsh, walks up to the stage to introduce Shania. With him is the president of PolyGram, Shania's label, who announces to the stunned audience that he has just been informed that her fourth CD has set a record as the biggest-selling album in the history of popular music. Released in the summer of 1999, it has already sold twenty-five million units worldwide. The audience erupts in applause.

A lone saxophone breaks through the melee, with a sultry solo that signals the start of the show. As the audience settles back into its chairs, the members of Shania's fifteen-piece band— drums, bass, lead guitar, two rhythm guitars, steel guitar, accordion, three fiddles, a saxophone, harmonica and three women backup singers—take their places. Shania walks out onstage, wearing a devastating black Dolce & Gabbana suit that fits her *like a second skin. She steps up to the microphone. "It's a real honor to be here tonight, with so many dear friends and colleagues. Tonight will be the biggest party night of the century, that's for sure."*

*For the next forty minutes, Shania performs many of the twelve number one hits that she's produced, along with her husband, Mutt, over the previous five years. As the clock approaches midnight, she steps up to the microphone to speak.*

*"I have only one wish for the world tonight. That we all make a personal commitment to make this planet a healthier, cleaner, safer and more loving place for our children." The audience breaks into a sincere round of applause.*

*Then Shania prepares to make another declaration. "Tonight," she says, "we are going to make a little music history." She suddenly giggles in a conspiratorial tone. "Now I know most of you expected just me and my band to perform for you tonight. I know there have been rumors over the past few weeks that a certain musician would be joining me tonight onstage, but I couldn't confirm that because, well, I've been busy. You know, getting things done before the end of the century." The audience laughs in unison.*

*"But it's true. I have managed to persuade my favorite American rocker, Bruce Springsteen, to join us tonight to ring in the next century." The crowd responds with pure enthusiasm as Bruce walks onstage. "And we might even play you that little single of ours that we recorded together earlier this year in New York. I want to thank all of you for helping take that song to number one on Billboard's rock, country, pop and R&B singles charts."*

*The band prepares to kick into a song, and as Bruce counts off "one-two-three-four," Shania looks out into the audience for the reassuring face of her husband. Then she begins to sing.*

◆  ◆  ◆

There are few who would dispute that Shania has earned her place as one of the most influential and successful recording artists in the history of country music, and perhaps in all of popular music. There are, however, many external forces that have contributed to Shania's success since the release of *The Woman in Me*—from the formidable growth of the country music industry since the late 1980s, to the aggressive international expansion of CMT, to the growing prominence and dominance of female country artists on the charts in the past five years. Though Shania is a fiercely independent musical tour de force, these trends within the country music industry deserve some exploration in order to better illuminate the story of Shania's success.

The music industry, like the stock market, has had its eras of booms and busts. In the mid-1980s, country music was experiencing one of the most serious busts—both creatively and sales-wise—in its sixty-five-year history. Country music was not growing. It was stagnant, and was not attracting new fans. Album sales were down, concert revenues were off, and despite the new medium called music videos, the genre lacked the sense of urgency or excitement that attracts a new audience. What was concerning many record label executives was the fact that the average country fan was fifty years old. This clearly indicated that younger fans—the major music consumers—were not joining the ranks of country music aficionados.

The CPR for country music came in the form of a dozen

or so hot, young male country artists who looked good and sounded better—Randy Travis, Dwight Yoakam, Vince Gill, Alan Jackson and George Strait, among them. For the next few years, country became a whole lot cooler, had more muscle and began luring younger fans into the fold. Then along came Garth Brooks.

Garth was the phenomenon that the country music industry was desperate for. The young Oklahoman introduced a bigger-than-life attitude to country music that made a lot of music consumers take notice. He not only produced solid country albums, but he performed them live, with the theatrics and energy of an arena rock act like Van Halen. Garth's 1989 self-titled debut album was well-received. His follow-up, *No Fences*, broke the sound barrier, becoming the biggest-selling country album in history, with thirteen million copies sold. *No Fences* spent twenty-three weeks at the top of the country charts and sold 700,000 copies within the first ten days of its release. His next three releases, *Ropin' the Wind, The Chase* and *In Pieces* all debuted at number one on both the *Billboard* Top 200 Albums chart and the *Billboard* Top 100 Country Albums chart. By 1998, the accumulated sales of his ten albums totaled close to sixty-five million copies, making him the biggest-selling country artist in history, and among the biggest-selling artists in all genres, even surpassing Elvis Presley. Only the Beatles, with 100 million albums, sold more records than Garth. His tenth album, *Sevens*, went gold (500,000 units sold) within the first few weeks of its release in November 1997. Like so many of his other previous efforts, *Sevens* debuted on the Top Country Albums and the Top 200 Albums charts at number one.

Garth's multimedia success does not stop at albums. In August 1997, he performed before an estimated 250,000 fans in Central Park in New York. The broadcast of the performance became the highest-rated original program on HBO that year.

The incredible turnaround in the country music scene, driven by power-country acts like Garth and by charismatic new-traditional artists like Randy Travis and Alan Jackson, brought a new sense of optimism to Nashville. Promising, innovative artists were signed in unprecedented numbers, and it was clear from label rosters that the young country fan was the target audience.

As more listeners began tuning in to the close to 2,500 country radio stations, record sales increased. Between 1989 and 1996, country music record sales quadrupled. Album sales and radio audiences were swelling not only in rural and small towns, but in urban areas. Twenty percent of the population of the major metropolitan areas in the United States were listening to country music every week. On a national level, more than forty-three million U.S. citizens were tuning in to country radio stations weekly, making it America's most popular music format.

Shania's music career was launched on the crest of this country music boom. She not only benefited from the industry's stellar growth, but she contributed to another seismic echo of the boom—the female invasion. In much the same fashion that the wave of male artists dominated the charts in the late 1980s and early 1990s, it is women who have taken over the radio and video channels in the second half of the 1990s.

In 1994, albums by women artists accounted for only

18.5 percent of all sales. By 1997 that figure had risen to 42.7 percent. In 1994 and 1995, Wynonna, Reba, Mary Chapin Carpenter, Alison Krauss, Shania and Trisha Yearwood dominated record sales among women artists. By 1998, there were dozens of new women country artists breaking into the world of platinum sales, including LeAnn Rimes, Deana Carter, and Martina McBride. The reason for the huge increase in women artists can be credited partly to programmers at country radio and video stations, who were responding to the demands of their female audience (their most prized listener in terms of advertising clout) for more female artists.

Although women artists claim close to 50 percent of all album sales in country music, there are still more male artists signed to recording contracts. Of the six artists who were responsible for selling 20 percent of all country albums between 1994 and 1997, five were men—Garth Brooks, Vince Gill, Alan Jackson, Tim McGraw and George Strait. The sole woman on the list was Reba McEntire.

It's Reba, newcomer LeAnn and Shania who are at the forefront of the female invasion. The three are so completely different from each other, in both musical and personal style, that it is almost absurd to compare them. But it is also hard to ignore the fact that the three are constantly jockeying for top position on the album and singles charts, vying for premium display space in the record stores, competing for the same industry awards and going after the same bookings on music awards and interview shows.

Reba has been the undisputed reigning queen of country music since the mid-1980s (she had an undistinguished career on Mercury Records in the late 1970s and early 1980s).

With eighteen albums to her credit, which have sold an accumulated thirty-five million copies, Reba has won every music award in the industry, including Grammys, American Music Awards, Academy of Country Music Awards and Country Music Association Awards. For years, no one came along with the celebrity clout to knock her off her pedestal—that is, until Shania arrived on the scene in 1995, and LeAnn Rimes in 1996. Shania outsold Reba in 1995, and in 1996 Shania and LeAnn were the two top-selling country artists, with Reba coming in a distant eighth. The two newcomers pulled the red carpet out from under Reba's feet, scoring almost every top music honor in 1996 and 1997.

Reba, however, is largely responsible for opening the door for the wave of independent and individualistic female country artists who arrived on the scene in the 1990s. She proved to an entire generation of women artists that they don't have to sit in the passenger seat when it comes to making decisions about their music and the management of their career. In 1984 she changed labels, moving to MCA, and in 1988 she really took the driver's seat when she launched Starstruck Entertainment. The multimedia corporation is headquartered in an imposing 25,000-square-foot glass office building and recording studio on Music Row which she owns with her husband and business partner, Narvel Blackstock. Starstruck Entertainment handles her bookings, management, publicity, travel and song publishing.

Reba's success is unprecedented in the music industry. Four of her albums have reached the triple platinum mark—*Read My Mind, It's Your Call, For My Broken Heart* and *Greatest Hits*—and one, *Greatest Hits II*, has sold four million copies. She has also scored high marks on tour. Her high-tech arena act was the top-grossing country tour in 1994, and in the top ten among concerts in all music styles. That year, her Thanksgiving special on NBC-TV was the highest-rated show in that time slot. Reba is also an accomplished television and movie actor, with credits that include roles in *North*, *The Little Rascals* and *The Man from Left Field.*

LeAnn Rimes (who is close to twenty-five years younger than Reba) showed up on the country music scene like Halley's Comet, and there were many who predicted that she would fade from view after her sensational debut album, *Blue.* But then came *Unchained Melody* and *Inspirational Songs* within a year and a half. All three releases peaked at number one on the *Billboard* Top 100 Country Albums chart, and they have sold a combined total of nine million albums. At fifteen, she became the youngest nominee in the history of the Country Music Association Awards, and in 1997 picked up the coveted Grammy awards for Best New Artist and Best Female Country Vocal Performance.

Born August 28, 1982, in Jackson, Mississippi, LeAnn gave her first public performance when she was five. She won a local song-and-dance competition with a rendition of "Getting to Know You." Her parents, Wilbur and Belinda, aggressively pursued a show business career for LeAnn for the next decade. They moved to Texas when she was six, because the music opportunities were greater there. At seven she made her theatrical debut in a Dallas musical production of *A Christmas Carol*, in the role of Tiny Tim. At eight, she won in the singing category on the national show *Star Search*. She became a regular on *Johnnie High's Country Music Review* in Fort Worth, Texas, performing hundreds of times in public by the time she was eleven. Her ambitious parents clearly felt it was her destiny to be a star, but it's easy to feel sympathetic toward a child who so obviously missed her childhood.

When LeAnn was eleven, her father and manager, Wilbur, produced her first album, *All That*, and released it on the independent label Nor Va Jak. The album featured the song "Blue," which would later be LeAnn's breakthrough single. Written by veteran songwriter Bill Mack, "Blue" had originally been written for Patsy Cline. But before she could record the yodel-rich song, she was killed in a plane crash.

LeAnn's album, *All That*, caught the attention of a number of record label executives in Nashville. Wilbur and Lyle Walker, who comanaged LeAnn's career, selected Curb Records, following a bidding war amongst several major labels. Curb made the unusual decision to release three CDs in less than two years, including *Unchained Melody*, a remastered version of *All That*.

The singles hit the charts like a hailstorm—"Blue," "One Way Ticket (Because I Can)," "How Do I Live?", "The Light in Your Eyes" and "On the Side of Angels." When her third album was released in August 1997, it debuted in the top spot on the country, pop and Christian charts, and earned her the distinction of being the first female artist in history to have three consecutive number one albums on the country charts. As if making records didn't keep her busy enough, LeAnn also produced a book, *Holiday in Your Heart*, with writer Tom Carter, and starred in the made-for-

TV movie that was based on it. And just to prove that wishes do come true, LeAnn's management sent her out on tour in 1997 (with chaperones, of course) with country's youngest male superstar, Bryan White.

In early 1998, the pendulum had swung back the other direction, and Reba won the fan-voted People's Choice Awards for favorite female performer (in a tie with Whitney Houston) and an American Music Award as Best Female Country Artist. Fans, it seems, are fickle and loyal at the same time.

There is no disputing that the 1990s have been dominated by the powerhouse careers of Shania, Garth, Reba and LeAnn, and these four artists will likely close out the century in the top five of the sales charts. And while there are dozens of exceptional country artists, both men and women, following close on their heels, there are few others who have scored close to perfect tens in all the categories that define a country superstar—hit records, multiple awards, high-impact videos, sold-out concerts and intense media attention.

Competing for sales and awards is not, at least consciously, on Shania's priority list. She claims that she is not a competitive person, and that she measures herself against her own performance standards, not those of others. Concentrating on sales figures, she says, takes the fun out of music.

It would be naive to assume that other country music artists share her nonchalant attitude toward competition. For many artists, rankings on *Billboard*'s charts and nominations for awards are a validation of one's talent and value in the music industry. The number one spot on the

*Billboard* Top Country Albums chart is a life goal for many artists, and when you're shut out by an album that's held that position for six months, there will undoubtedly be some sour grapes. When *The Woman in Me* dominated the top of the country charts for a significant portion of 1995 and 1996, it caused many other artists' albums to hit the ceiling at number two before slipping back down the ratings ladder. Garth's album *The Hits* was number one when Shania arrived on the scene in July 1995, and she unceremoniously bumped him out of the top spot. His album would never have the chance to become a long-term number one hit, because by the time Shania was shaken loose from that spot by Brooks and Dunn, and later by LeAnn Rimes's album, *Blue,* Garth's album had peaked (his label released *The Hits* for a special limited time to push sales and create a demand for the album). Although Garth's anthology would eventually sell over eight million albums, it did it primarily as a top five hit, not a number one. In November 1995, Garth released *Fresh Horses*, his first album of new material in two years. Though it made a stop at number one, its stay was relatively short, due to the ongoing sales strength of *The Woman in Me.* Shania was firmly planted at the top for most of the first half of 1996, as she rode the wave of three consecutive number one singles.

There is one record, however, which Garth holds that may be impossible for Shania to break—in 1993, he sold out the 65,000-seat Texas Stadium for concerts on three consecutive nights. It was the largest audience ever in country music history.

In 1996, Shania Twain was voted the Best Country Female Artist at the American Music Awards. At the 1997

AMAs, LeAnn Rimes excitedly clutched the trophy for Favorite New Country Artist—her first major award. In 1998, Reba received the AMA honor as Best Country Female Artist. Only time will tell if Shania, LeAnn and Reba will continue to alternate sweeping every awards show into the year 2000, before being challenged by one of the many talented women in country music who are quietly waiting in the wings to make their move.

There have been few discernible changes in Shania's public persona between the time she released *The Woman in Me* in February 1995 and *Come on Over* in November 1997. She continued to project herself in public as a woman who is confident in her musical vision, comfortable with her body and content with her professional and personal life with her producer and husband, Mutt Lange. What has changed dramatically is her broadening involvement in the world outside of the "Twain Zone." From 1987 through 1992, she was driven by such domestic needs as looking after her parents' estate, raising her brothers and sister, and making ends meet. When she landed her record deal with Mercury Nashville and released her debut album in 1993, her focus shifted to her musical needs—recording and performing songs. After meeting and marrying Mutt, her focal point became the development of her musical voice, as both a singer and a songwriter. With Mutt's support, she flourished as a songwriter, gained confidence in the studio and emerged as a more self-assured performer. In the post–*Woman in Me* era, Shania found herself financially, emotionally and professionally secure for the first time in her life.

Mutt, who is as much at home in Europe as he is in

North America, introduced Shania to new experiences in the far reaches of the world. Walking along a beach in Southern France, watching a soccer game in a stadium in Italy, visiting her in-laws in South Africa and other such experiences opened Shania to the global village, and it has had an impact on her musical life.

The final single to be released from *The Woman in Me* was an expanded version of "God Bless the Child." This poignant song was the soothing lullaby that Shania used to sing to herself after her parents died. When she performed the song at the 1996 Country Music Awards, she was accompanied by the African-American gospel group Take Six and a multicultural children's choir, who were also featured in her video. The song, which speaks to the victimization of children in all its forms—including sexual abuse, neglect and poverty—demonstrated Shania's commitment to using her music to address serious social issues. The proceeds from the sale of the single were donated to the Second Harvest/Kids Cafe program in the United States. In Canada, she has contributed generously to the Canadian Living Foundation's Breakfast for Learning. Her donation was a gracious and humble gesture which signaled a new philanthropic side of Shania. She once told a reporter that she has a hard time eating large quantities of food, because so many children go without in the world. If she truly wants to demonstrate her compassion for the less fortunate, she'll continue on this path, and not let this be an isolated gesture designed to garner maximum media exposure.

Shania has said that her songs frequently reflect her true convictions and attitudes. She told *Country Weekly* magazine, "There's nothing on this album [*Come on Over*] I wouldn't stand by lyrically. A lot of subject matter on this album goes deeper for me personally than I portray in the songs, because obviously I'm trying to entertain people and not get all heavy on them."

She has also said that with *Come on Over*, she has found a new sense of freedom. She has carved out her own niche in the music world, and fans, music critics and music industry insiders have no alternative but to accept what she chooses to create musically.

To Shania, songs are windows into a songwriter's soul and personality. Songs like "Any Man of Mine," and "Honey, I'm Home" use humor—a device frequently present in her music—to express her conviction that women are special, and deserve a certain amount of pampering in a relationship. This does not mean that the attention should be a one-way street; however, it is clear that the female characters in both songs expect some return on their investment.

Many of her songs support a woman's right to be in a relationship that fulfills her needs. "Black Eyes, Blue Tears" describes a woman who is getting out of a physically abusive relationship, and "Leavin' Is the Only Way Out" describes a relationship that has dissolved into anger and pain and is no longer worth sacrificing for.

The vast majority of Shania's songs reveal her healthy obsession with romance. Shania is a woman who not only believes in romance, but insists that it is the key ingredient in making a relationship work. Shania's fascination with love and romance is the driving force behind many songs on her third release, *Come on Over*. She is not the least bit self-conscious about standing by her man, or expecting and giving unconditional love.

"Love Gets Me Every Time," the first single released, is ironic in that the love-struck woman in the song never really wanted to be that way at all—she'd been content "paying my own rent." The song delivers the signature independent spirit of "Any Man of Mine," with the giddy acceptance of hopeless love à la "No One Needs to Know" or "I'm Holding on to Love (to Save My Life)." Fans obviously liked the song's tension between independence and freedom. It arrived at number 20 on the Top 100 Country Singles, making it the highest debut ever by a female country artist. The song reached number one in six weeks.

On occasion, Shania takes idyllic love to the extreme, such as in her pledge to "give my last breath" to her lover in the song "From This Moment On." The custom-made wedding song features Shania and Bryan White in the album's sole duet. In fact, Bryan's is the only voice, other than Shania's and Mutt's, featured in *Come on Over*.

The most unusual transition between the songs on *The Woman in Me* and those on *Come on Over* is that the latter is peppered with trendy, often passé, clichés and references to a youthful pop culture. Mentions include Dr. Ruth, the Internet, PMS, Brad Pitt, CNN, Elvis and the Beatles. Though these are certainly icons of our media-saturated world, they come across as somewhat trite in her songs. If Shania wants her songs to endure, she might limit the number of songs that resort to playful, but meaningless, clichés. They appear so often in her songs that they begin to take away from the depth of the music by placing them into the novelty-song category. This is hardly the way to create classics.

*Come on Over* carried the burden of having to compete against its successful predecessor, *The Woman in Me*, and its history-making thirteen million sales. Shania and Mutt retreated to the recording studio at their upstate New York estate in late 1996 to take on that challenge. They ultimately wrote and recorded twenty songs, then chose sixteen tracks for the album. When Shania announced that she would not perform at Fan Fair '97, in order to continue working on her album, the news disappointed hundreds of her fans who had already purchased tickets to see her perform live in Nashville that June. But the pressure of making a fall deadline (the release date was changed more than once) kept the Langes focused.

When the album was released, it received respectful, but mixed, reviews. *Billboard*, in its November 1997 issue, said, "In a very real sense, this is the future of power pop merging with country. In the process, country's traditions are being reinvented and redefined."

*Rolling Stone* was not as kind: "The first thing you notice about Shania Twain's *Come on Over*, once you get past her pretty pictures on the cover, is how the titles have way too many exclamation points: 'Man! I Feel Like a Woman!' 'Whatever You Do! Don't!'. So does the music. . . . On *Come on Over*, their songs are speedier and more concise, hopped up on the exact same sassy little chassis of synthesized sound and bim-bam-boom bleacher beats that Lange pioneered on '80s records by Def Leppard and the Cars."

Shania's fans, however, embraced the album with unbridled enthusiasm. Within two months of its release, it had gone triple platinum (three million sales). The master plan for *Come on Over* is clearly international saturation.

This was also the plan for *The Woman in Me,* but that album never enjoyed the worldwide release of *Come on Over.* When her second release became a power hit in 1995, any global plans were set aside in an attempt to satisfy the insatiable appetite for Shania in Canada and the United States. *Come on Over* was remixed by Mutt for an international market, and was released in early 1998 as a pop, as opposed to a country, album. There's no doubt, however, that the international CMTs will figure prominently in its promotion. Shania's 1998–99 world tour will include stops in Europe, Australia, the Pacific Rim and Latin America.

Shania's live concert tour has more than delivered on her promise of high-energy, every-night-is-a-party live show but it intentionally does not resemble halftime at the Super Bowl. Her songs are all the "flash" she needs in her concerts, with state-of-the-art sound and light systems designed to bring out the best live performance possible.

She's been anxious to perform live, something that she hasn't done since her "Triple Play" tour in 1993. Even though she has appeared countless times on television since 1995, Shania doesn't consider these shows to represent anything close to performing "live." In fact, she often appears less than comfortable on programs like *Late Show with David Letterman, Live! . . . With Regis & Kathie Lee* and *The Tonight Show with Jay Leno.* The closest she has gotten to a full-out "rock this country" show has been her appearances at Fan Fair from 1993 through 1996. Some of her performances at awards shows, such as the 1995 *Billboard* Awards and the 1996 American Music Awards, have hinted at what Shania is capable of offering in concert. In both cases, she performed in front of large audiences (at the New York City Coliseum and the Shrine Auditorium).

Her new nine-piece band, noticeably "younger" and perhaps initially less confident than her 1995–96 band, includes drums, bass, lead guitar, steel guitar, two guitarists (not including Shania) and three fiddle players. Shania and her band have a twenty-eight-song repertoire from her last two releases to draw from, and there's little doubt that her audience will know every word to every song that she performs. Imagine a 20,000-voice-strong choir helping her out with the chorus, and you get the idea.

The song that is destined to become the flagship anthem on her world concert tour is "Rock This Country." It's the type of song that will be sung en masse at concerts, and that will be remembered by thousands as "that song that we played full blast on our car stereo during the summer of 1998." Shania also gives women their own theme song, "Man! I Feel Like a Woman!". It has all the ingredients to become the most requested "girls night out" song off the album. It's Shania's way of saying to women, "Get out there and have some fun—we deserve it."

Shania designed her own custom touring bus, which is her second home on the American and Canadian portions of the tour. Also along for the tour are her horse, an Appaloosa, and her dog, Tim.

Part of the musical confidence and spontaneity on *Come on Over* is the result of Shania's maturing relationship with Mutt. When they made their first album together, they were just getting to know each other, both in a musical sense, as songwriters, and on a personal level, as a newly married couple. By 1997, when they were recording their second project together, they had been together for four years. Any inhibitions that they'd had working together in 1993 and 1994 had disappeared, and this new comfort zone is evident in the songs.

The experience of writing songs for her latest release was also different from *The Woman in Me,* which included many songs that were written when the couple were traveling in Europe. Most of *Come on Over* emerged from songwriting sessions at their estate near Lake Placid, some of which extended for several days. Shania describes a typical session: "Sometimes we would literally go two or three days at a time where we'd sit by the fire and start writing in the morning, go for a walk later in the afternoon, go for a horseback ride or eat, then write, go to bed really late, get up in the morning and start all over again."

The song "From This Moment On" was written far from their woodland retreat, however. Shania wrote this song in Italy, while sitting in a stadium watching a soccer game with Mutt, who happens to love the sport. While he followed the action on the playing field, Shania quietly worked on the lyrics for the song. Her original plan was to put the song in her publishing catalog and perhaps find another singer to record it in the future. Mutt persuaded her to record it on *Come on Over* as a duet. Her first choice for the duet was Bryan White.

Though Bryan is ten years younger than Shania, they exude the same youthful exuberance and playfulness in their videos and in real life. Bryan landed his recording contract with Asylum when he was nineteen years old, at about the same time that Shania was launching her career with Mercury Nashville. In fact, Bryan and Shania were both nominated for a CMA Horizon Award in 1996 (Bryan took home the trophy that night).

There are other similarities between the two singers. Both are prolific songwriters—Shania records only her own and Mutt's material, and many of the songs on Bryan's albums are his own. Both artists come from musical families, and were nurtured by parents who supported their choice of careers. Bryan got a set of drums at five, but switched to guitar when he was a teenager.

Bryan and Shania both came to Nashville to pursue music careers right out of high school. Bryan stayed to pay his dues, while Shania returned to Timmins to continue developing her performing and songwriting skills. Bryan was fortunate to have caught the attention of the same publishing company that helped launch Alan Jackson's career, Glen Campbell Music and GC Management, as well as the ears of Kyle Lehning and Billy Joe Walker Jr., two prominent Nashville producers who would eventually become Bryan's coproducers. Kyle told him to concentrate on his writing skills for a year before pursuing a recording contract.

Both Shania and Bryan have released three albums, and each have a string of number one hits to their credit. Perhaps most important, both have demonstrated their commitment to helping out youth and community programs. Bryan, who is originally from Oklahoma, raised $75,000 for an education fund for the children orphaned and injured in the 1995 Oklahoma City bombing. He has supported the Cerebral Palsy Foundation, the T. J. Martell Foundation, the Cystic Fibrosis Foundation, "Country CARES," the Native American Clothing Drive and St. Jude Children's Research

Hospital. Shania's favorite causes involve youth and food banks.

To break the ice when Bryan arrived to record the duet, Shania took him horseback riding on her and Mutt's 3,000-acre estate. Then, feeling more comfortable with each other, they went into the studio and recorded the classic "From This Moment On."

Though her musical partnership with Bryan is a highlight on the album, it is her ongoing collaboration with Mutt that dominates every song. Shania has stated that some of the songs on *Come on Over* are autobiographical, including "You're Still the One" and "Come on Over." In both songs, she writes about her relationship with Mutt. The songs are Shania's way of responding to rumors that their marriage is on shaky ground. She used the songs to reaffirm her love and relationship with Mutt, both on a personal and public level.

The musical and personal magic between Shania and Mutt has resulted in an album that offers an intimate look at what makes Shania tick. The collaboration confidently offers Shania's musical worldview—her music, lyrics and stories are as sincere, romantic and exuberant as she is.

If *The Woman in Me* is any indicator, the expected life span of *Come on Over* will be at least two years. Shania has announced that she will release ten singles off the album. With strong album sales and consistently high-charting singles, the album could come close to achieving the success of *The Woman in Me*.

After only six years as a recording artist, Shania holds the distinction of being one of only five female artists to have sold ten million copies of an album in the United

States. The other albums are Alanis Morissette's *Jagged Little Pill* (fifteen million), Whitney Houston's self-titled debut (twelve million), Carole King's *Tapestry* (ten million) and Mariah Carey's *Music Box* (ten million).

*The Woman in Me* is only the fourth country album to ever break the ten-million mark. Garth Brooks and Kenny Rogers are the only other members in this exclusive "ten million sales" club. Despite stellar careers, Reba, Trisha, Wynonna and LeAnn come nowhere close to Shania in terms of number of albums sold.

Shania has often cited her major musical influences when she was growing up—Loretta Lynn, Dolly Parton and Karen Carpenter are among them. There is one artist whom Shania has never mentioned, but who shares some interesting career similarities. That artist is Patsy Cline, who Shania eclipsed as the biggest-selling female country artist in 1996 (Patsy's album of greatest hits has sold six million copies, the previous record).

Patsy, like Shania, had one foot in country and the other in pop music, and she was frequently criticized for her refusal to choose one over the other. Patsy's albums were a seesaw of musical styles, and she seemed destined to keep both of her audiences happy.

Patsy's peers, however, had no qualms about honoring her for her contributions to both music styles. She received numerous awards, including *Billboard*'s Favorite Female Artist, *Cash Box*'s Most Programmed C&W Female and Most Programmed Album of the Year, the *Music Reporter*'s Star of the Year and Female Vocalist of the Year and *Music Vendor*'s Female Vocalist of the Year.

Shania, like Patsy, is uninhibited in expressing her sexuality and her zest for life. The two have both been subject to the whispered condemnation of having taken their "female attributes" too far.

It is the similarities between two songs that offer the most striking link between the two singers—Shania's "Come on Over" and Patsy's "Come on In."

Shania's song features the lyrics, "Come on over, come on in/Pull up a seat, take a load off your feet . . . When you're up, when you're down/When you need a laugh come around." Shania has mentioned to music journalists that it is one of her favorite songs.

Patsy frequently sang "Come on In" (written by V. F. Stewart) in her live shows, and referred to it as one of her favorite songs. The song goes: "When I'd go over to my neighbor's house/Knock on the door and they'd all sing out/Come on in and sit right down and make yourself at home."

Though Shania's and Patsy's musical careers are separated by forty years of time, they share an affection for songs that celebrate the down-home, pull-up-a-chair friendliness that makes both singers such appealing musical phenomena.

Shania once said, "It's your songs, not your celebrity, that will give you your longevity." Patsy has clearly proven that songs are an artist's most enduring legacy. Shania takes it a step further. By being both the writer and performer of her songs, she is able to bring to life both her musical and personal points of view.

In the final analysis, it becomes irrelevant whether

Shania uses rock or country or zydeco to express her musical vision. It's far more significant that her songs bring a little romance, humor and exuberance into the lives of millions of people every day.

# APPENDIX

SHANIA TWAIN DISCOGRAPHY
*Albums*
*Shania Twain* 1993
*The Woman in Me* 1995
*Come on Over* 1997

*Singles*
"What Made You Say That" 1993
"Dance with the One That Brought You" 1993
"You Lay a Whole Lot of Love on Me" 1993
"Whose Bed Have Your Boots Been Under?" 1995
"Any Man of Mine" 1995
"The Woman in Me (Needs the Man in You)" 1995
"(If You're Not in It for Love) I'm Outta Here" 1995
"You Win My Love" 1996
"No One Needs to Know" 1996
"Home Ain't Where His Heart Is (Anymore)" 1996
"God Bless the Child" 1996
"Love Gets Me Every Time" 1997
"Don't Be Stupid (You Know I Love You)" 1997
"You're Still the One" 1998
"From This Moment On" 1998
"Honey I'm Home" 1998

VIDEO COMPILATIONS
*Shania Twain* 1995
*The Complete Woman in Me* 1996

AWARDS
1998 Juno: Country Female Vocalist
1997 Juno: Country Female Vocalist
1997 Juno: International Achievement
1996 Juno: Country Female Vocalist
1996 Juno: Entertainer of the Year
1996 Canadian Country Music Association: Female Vocalist of the Year
1996 CCMA Fans' Choice Entertainer of the Year
1996 CCMA Video of the Year—"(If You're Not in It for Love) I'm Outta Here"
1996 Billboard Music Award: Country Album of the Year—*The Woman in Me*
1996 Academy of Country Music: Top New Female Vocalist
1996 ACM: Album of the Year—*The Woman in Me*
1996 Grammy: Best Country Album—*The Woman in Me*
1996 Blockbuster Entertainment Awards: Favorite New Country Artist
1996 Great British Country Music Awards: International Rising Star
1996 Country Music Television/Europe: Female Artist of the Year
1996 Country Music Television/Europe: Video of the Year—"Any Man of Mine"
1996 World Music Awards: World's Best Selling Female Country Artist
1995 American Music Awards: Favorite New Country Artist
1995 CCMA: Single of the Year—"Any Man of Mine"
1995 CCMA: Album of the Year—*The Woman in Me*
1995 CCMA: Socan Song of the Year—"Whose Bed Have Your Boots Been Under?"
1995 CCMA: Female Vocalist of the Year
1995 CCMA: Video of the Year—"Any Man of Mine"
1995 RPM's Big Country Awards: Outstanding New Artist
1993 Country Music Television/Europe: Rising Star

MILESTONES

August 28, 1965: Born in Windsor, Ontario, to Clarence and Sharon Edwards

1968: Clarence and Sharon separate. Sharon moves to Timmins, Ontario

1971: Sharon marries Jerry Twain, an Ojibwa from Timmins

1973: Eilleen begins singing in public, including community centers, senior citizen homes and the Mattagami Hotel lounge

1974: Performs duets with Lawrence Martin, an Ojibwa singer (now recording on First Nations Records)

1978: Appears on *The Tommy Hunter Show* in Toronto

1983: Graduates from Timmins High and Vocational School

1984: Plays in the band Longshot in the Timmins area

1984–1987: Works at family reforestation company during the summers. Plays in bands on the weekends and in the winters.

1987: Performs at Canadian Native Arts Foundation's gala, as opening act for Bernadette Peters and the Toronto Symphony

1987: Jerry and Sharon are killed in a car accident

1987: Eilleen becomes guardian of her two brothers and one sister, and executor of her parents' estate

1988–1991: Eilleen moves family to Huntsville, Ontario, where she works as a singer and performer in the Deerhurst Resort's dinner theater and *Viva Vegas* show

1991: Eilleen changes her name to Shania, which means "I'm on my way" in Ojibwa. Shania is the name of a costume assistant with whom Eilleen worked at Deerhurst.

1991: Dick Frank, a Nashville entertainment lawyer, comes to Deerhurst, at the invitation of manager Mary Bailey, to see Shania perform

1991: Shania signs a recording contract with Mercury Nashville and moves to Nashville to record a demo tape

1992: Shania records her debut album at the Music Mill Studio in Nashville with Harold Shedd and Norro Wilson coproducing

1993: Shania's self-titled debut album is released

1993: *Shania Twain* peaks at #68 on the *Billboard* Top Country Albums chart

1993: First single to reach the *Billboard* Hot Country Singles chart, "What Made You Say That," peaks at #55

1993: Second single to reach the *Billboard* Hot Country Singles chart, "Dance with the One That Brought You," peaks at #55

1993: Shania meets Robert John "Mutt" Lange in person at Fan Fair in Nashville

1993: Shania and Mutt are married on December 28 in Huntsville

1995: Second CD, *The Woman in Me*, is released in February

1995: "Whose Bed Have Your Boots Been Under?" peaks at #11

1995: First #1 single, "Any Man of Mine"

1996: Second #1 single, "(If You're Not in It for Love) I'm Outta Here"

1996: Third #1 single, "You Win My Love"

1996: Fourth #1 single, "No One Needs to Know"

1997: *The Woman in Me* is certified as selling nine million copies in the United States and an additional three million worldwide

1997: Shania and Mutt record *Come on Over* in New York, Nashville, Mamaroneck and Toronto

1997: First #1 single from *Come on Over*, "Love Gets Me Every Time"

1997: Shania's third CD, *Come on Over*, is released on November 4

1998: "Don't Be Stupid (You Know I Love You)," peaks at #6

1998: "You're Still the One," peaks at #1

1998: "From This Moment On," peaks at #6


All chart statistics are from *Billboard* magazine

SHANIA FACTS
Weight: 110
Height: 5' 4"
Eyes: Brown
Hair: Brown
Shoe Size: 6½
Favorite Food: Pasta
Favorite Dessert: All pastries, but especially peach pie
Favorite Colors: Red, green

Favorite Music: Everything
Favorite Songs: "Wildflower" (Skylarc); "Dream a Little Dream of Me" (Mamas & Papas); "Coat of Many Colors" and "In the Ghetto" (Dolly Parton); "She's Always a Woman to Me" (Billy Joel); "I'm So Lonesome I Could Cry" (Hank Williams)
Favorite Recreation: Canoeing, camping, horseback riding
Favorite Instrument: Guitar
First Performance: First-grade show-and-tell—sang John Denver's "Country Roads"

# EXCERPTS FROM
# TWO INTERVIEWS
# WITH SHANIA TWAIN

On April 21 and April 23, 1996, Barbara Hager interviewed Shania Twain for a book that she was writing about successful Native Canadians. The book, *Honour Song: A Tribute,* was published by Raincoast Books in 1996 and includes a chapter on Shania. The following are excerpts from two conversations she had with Shania—a telephone interview on April 21 and an in-person interview with her on April 23 at Universal Studios in Los Angeles.

Telephone interview with Shania Twain
April 21, 1996

Barbara Hager (BH): Thanks for taking the time to talk with me, Shania. Whatever we don't get to today, I hope we can talk about on Tuesday, when we meet in person in L.A.
Shania Twain (ST): That sounds great. Since it's Sunday, it's a fairly quiet day for me, so this is a good time to talk.
BH: Patty Lou may have told you that I'm writing a book about Native Canadian achievers. I'm hoping that the book will offer young people some Native role models who have been successful in their careers. I'm interviewing sixteen peo-

ple for the book, including singer Susan Aglukark; Ted Nolan, who's the coach of the Buffalo Sabres; Angela Chalmers, the Olympic runner; and Graham Greene, who was in *Dances with Wolves.*

Today, I'd like to talk mainly about your music career as a child and teenager in Timmins. I'd also like to talk about how you've been influenced by your father's Aboriginal culture.

So let's start at the very beginning. Can you recall the very first song that you sang as a child?

ST: I distinctly remember singing when I was three years old. I would go off by myself and sing a song like "Twinkle, Twinkle," changing the rhythm and humming different tones. My mother was listening to me, but I didn't know it at the time.

BH: Who first noticed that you had musical talent?

ST: Both my mom and dad. My parents loved music, and there was always music being played in the house and in their truck.

BH: Were your parents musical? Are there any musicians in your family?

ST: My father played a little guitar, and he taught me a few chords. He played mostly Stompin' Tom Connors songs. A few of my cousins played instruments. One of my dad's cousins played in a family band with me when I was about ten years old. I grew up as the "singer in the family." To the rest of the community, I was the "Twain Girl."

BH: Where did you perform as a child?

ST: I would perform on the telethons and at family parties. My mom would take me to sing for my Great-grandpa Twain at the senior citizen home where he lived. My mom would arrange for me to sing at parks, at community centers, at hospitals. When we lived in Sudbury, I played at the Northern Lights Festival. For a while I teamed up with Lawrence Martin [now a Native recording artist in Canada], and we sang as a duo at talent contests around Ontario.

From the time that I was eight, my parents would wake me up in the middle of the night to take me out to sing at clubs with bands, after they'd stopped selling liquor. I wasn't comfortable being woken up. But my parents were really into music, and they had a concept of a music career for me. They discovered my talent, and wanted to expose me to a musical environment.

BH: Did you enjoy music as a child?

ST: I have fond memories of music. When I was young, I liked music in the same way other girls might like playing with Barbies. I was introduced to a career and responsibilities when I was quite young. It wasn't just a hobby.

I do remember having stage fright as a child, but I learned that children can face their fears. I never shied away from music. I was a very serious songwriter from an early age.

When I was a kid, music wasn't something that I aspired to. I didn't think that I would grow up to be a singer. I was already a singer.

BH: Did both parents encourage you, or was one the main "stage parent"?

ST: My mom was more of the stage parent. My dad was more practical. He made decisions about whether it made sense to drive somewhere to perform for free, or to pay the heating bill that week. Once my father decided that we couldn't afford to travel to a certain town to perform. After I went to bed that night, I snuck out of my window and my mom and I went anyway.

Everyone has a talent. I'm lucky that my parents recognized mine and helped me do something with it. There was never any doubt in my parents' minds that I was going to become a successful musician.

BH: Who were your musical influences?

ST: Karen Carpenter. Dolly Parton was a big influence. She grew up poor like me. Her song "Coat of Many Colors" was a big inspiration. I thought, If she can do it, so can I.

BH: How did your teachers and classmates relate to your career?

ST: My teachers took my music seriously. They'd always grant me time out when I needed it, like when I had to go to Toronto for *The Tommy Hunter Show.*

I remember once, when I was in grade five, being asked to perform at a parent-teacher program. The principal had heard that I was a singer and he asked if I could perform for this program. I remember telling him that I would need a microphone, a monitor and a sound system. He didn't know how to respond. Then I told him to call my mother to schedule the performance. For some reason the performance didn't take place, but it was pretty obvious that I was a professional singer even at that age.

BH: Did you go through the typical rebellious teenaged phase where you turned away from your parents?

ST: I escaped that phase because of my music. I was too busy for that. In high school I played in bands every weekend. I didn't drink because it wasn't something that you did when you were working. I missed my high school graduation ceremony because I had to get on the road with my band.

BH: What was it like growing up in northern Canada?

ST: I spent a lot of time outdoors when I was growing up. We camped out a lot. Not in campgrounds, but out in the bush, or near an uninhabited lake my father knew about. We would just sleep in the back of the truck or pitch a canvas tent somewhere.

My parents had a trapline, and my dad and brothers trapped and hunted. We ate rabbit and partridge, and sometimes we'd get moose meat from my dad's reservation.

My dad started a tree-planting business when I was in high school, so every summer for several years, I worked for him. It was a real family business. My grandparents worked in the camp kitchen, my aunt kept the books back in Timmins, my mom looked after things in camp and my father ran the forest operations. I was a crew foreman, and I had an all-Native staff from Moose Factory, Moosonee and Manitoulin Island.

BH: Were you close to your grandparents on your father's side? Did your grandparents share any of their traditional Ojibwa skills with you?

ST: My grandparents taught me how to track and snare rabbits. They would take me out into the bush in winter and show me where the rabbits' tracks would intersect. That's where you'd set up your snare. Trapping was part of our lifestyle when I was growing up. It was about surviving.

BH: There's been some controversy in the media lately about your Aboriginal heritage. How is this affecting your sense of identity?

ST: Being Native is not something that I became. It's something that I've always been. If you were adopted into an Italian family, you would grow up with those traditions and values and sense of family.

I was adopted by my Ojibwa father, and that's the culture that I grew up in. My grandparents spoke Ojibwa, and I spent a lot of time with them.

I don't feel any different than my brothers. I grew up in a Native family, and don't see myself in any other way. After the media started covering this, I got calls from my father's family. They've said to me, You're one of us, and don't let anyone take that away from you.

There are people who are trying to challenge that, but I already know who I am, and who my family is. It's too late to end that mind-set.

BH: I grew up in a large family myself, with a Native father and a non-Native mother. I remember being exposed to racism as a child. Did you experience this growing up?

ST: I encountered racism growing up. Sometimes we were the only Native family in our neighborhood. I stuck up for myself and my brothers. There was one time when I was in my teens and the parents of a boy I was dating made him stop seeing me because I was Native.

BH: You're well-known in the Aboriginal community, but you don't identify yourself as a Native performer in the bigger entertainment world.

ST: I've never used my heritage to get ahead in the music business. My father used to tell us to pursue success as individuals. He told us not to use being Native to get something, or to get special treatment.

I don't use my Native heritage as part of my identity as a musician. But I remember my mom and dad used to laugh at me when I was a kid playing country music. My dad would say I was playing both the cowboy and the Indian because I'd wear a buckskin jacket and cowboy boots.

BH: You have a lot of fans in the Aboriginal community. Do you stay in touch with your Aboriginal roots now?

ST: For history's sake, and community's sake, it's important to stay in touch with your culture. But I've chosen to keep my Native identity separate from my music career. In fact, I didn't realize growing up that there was a larger Native community. But I'm really pleased by the support I'm getting from Native people in Canada and the United States.

In-person interview with Shania Twain
April 23, 1996

Barbara Hager (BH): Thanks, Shania, for taking time out of your crazy schedule so that I can interview you for my book. I thought we'd pick up where we left off when we talked on the phone the other day. We talked a lot about your family and your early childhood. I'd like to talk about your life after you moved to Huntsville to work at Deerhurst. I think that you had mentioned that Mary Bailey was helping you get through a very difficult time in your life after your parents died in a highway accident.

Shania Twain (ST): Mary Bailey was very encouraging. After my parents died, I decided that . . . well, I wasn't decided about anything. I didn't know what I was going to do. I knew that I had to be there for my family. And I was going to make that commitment. That's when Mary said, What are you going to do about singing? I said, I really cannot see me, at this point, pursuing a career. I've got two brothers that I've got to take care of. I became the executor for the estate. I had to sell my parents' home, sell their business and all their equipment. I had to deal with their taxes. And I had to deal with my brothers' insurance because they were orphans and my one brother was in the accident so there were settlements there. It was very complex. And there was no will. So I really had to accept that responsibility.

BH: Twenty-two is not an age when most people normally deal with those types of responsibilities.

ST: That's an age when you're just trying to figure out what you want. I thought to myself, I was either going to escape it all, and go off to Africa or dig in and deal with it. For some reason I wanted to go to Africa. I had this idea of going as far away as I could. I wanted to go somewhere where civilization was so different that I could escape everything that was happening. I ended up staying and coping with the responsibility.

Mary, of course, was concerned about my career. She said, You know, you can't just quit singing. But I didn't know what to do. I said, I don't have a choice. She said, Why don't you come [with me] to Deerhurst.

BH: This was the first time you'd ever been to Deerhurst?

ST: This was right at the point where I was just beginning to deal with my parents' affairs. She said, Why don't you just come for a trip, drive up with me. Maybe this will give you some inspiration. It ended up I went in there and I sang in the lounge with one of the acts there, and they basically hired me on the spot to be in the show. Of course, in discussing that I said, Well, you know, I have a family. It's not like I was this free soul. They were surprised when I told them that I had a family to support. I asked how stable it was because I had to uproot my family [from Timmins]. It turned out to be very stable. I was under contract, and the salary was good enough that I could buy a home.

BH: It was just like when you were ten years old and you were telling the principal that you had to have a monitor, and you had to have a microphone . . .

ST: Exactly. It's the story of my life, isn't it? I've always had to be ahead of my years. But it was a great experience, when I look back at it now.

BH: It probably stabilized you for a while. You didn't have to go on the road.

ST: It made me stationary for a while, which is what my music career [in a band] would normally not have done. So I was able to have a musical career, and especially a musical education because it was something so out of the ordinary for me. I would not normally have been in a Broadway revue.

BH: Different range of music, dance . . .

ST: Dancing, singing, movement, group singing, a bit of acting, musical theater. It was really, really great.

BH: Did it help your confidence [as a performer]?

ST: Amazingly so. I was experiencing something totally new. Of course, here was this singer, who for the most part, up until I was fifteen years old, really didn't sing much without my guitar. I was always behind my guitar.

BH: It was a security blanket.

ST: Yeah. Even when I did some rock, which was what I did for a while. I put my guitar down a bit for that. But I still felt more comfortable with it. Until I went to Deerhurst and they said, No way, you're not taking out your guitar.

BH: Was it like a performing arts school?

ST: It was almost like a musical education. I always had a dream of going to a performing arts school, and in some ways, that's what Deerhurst gave me. I actually really cherished that time. Even though it was probably the three most difficult years of my life, because it was obviously after my parents' death. I was trying to cope with my two teenage brothers, I was trying to pay a mortgage, I'm trying to deal with their finances and also dealing with my parents' taxes. That was stuff that had to be taken care of. I didn't know the first thing about all that. I learned very quickly.

BH: Do you feel now that you have people looking after a lot of your business, that maybe now you can focus on your musical career?

ST: Right now I'm going through the most dependent period of my entire life. I've never depended on people as much as I am now. It's a very vulnerable feeling. First of all, being a celebrity, people find out where you're staying. Even to go down to the corner store I have to call someone to go with me. I feel like such a burden.

BH: Have you lost some independence and spontaneity in your life now that you're a celebrity?

ST: I am not a child. I can go do things independently. Even when I was a child, I was more independent. That's why I got my dog, Tim. I can go for a little stroll sometimes, without everyone being worried about me.

BH: There must be a whole thing about the psychology of being a celebrity in America. How does it feel to be recognized on the street and in public?

ST: It's very strange. I knew that it was going to come if I was ever to become successful. I'm not complaining about it, because I do enjoy it. But I'm the kind of person who has to find a way to be comfortable and satisfied. Having Tim is one answer. I definitely disguise myself sometimes, if I don't want to be mobbed. Anything for my independence.

BH: It seems like you have a good team around you.

ST: Yes, I do. I depend on a lot of people. You can't do all the jobs yourself. You have to have people that you trust to do certain jobs for you. You have to allow for that.

BH: It's not like when you were twenty-two having to look after everything.

ST: I was a control freak then.

BH: You live in a remote area now, in upstate New York. That must give you some privacy.

ST: I enjoy living in a secluded area where I really don't have to worry about what I look like or what I'm wearing. The people are normal, everyday people, like the people that I grew up with. I enjoy that. Being at home is like a freedom.

BH: I want to switch gears a little and talk about your music. Your lyrics are really different for country songs. They're not your classic country songs where the woman is often the victim, or at least the man has control of the relationship. Is that an extension of your independence?

ST: That's definitely me. It's basically my personality coming out in my lyrics. My husband is partly responsible for that because he encourages it in me. I haven't always been brave enough to say some of the things I've said through my songs. I'll show him a song, and he'll say, You've got to say it like it is. Be yourself. So I come up with all these lyrics that are, well, fun and independent.

BH: I've read somewhere that you said that you aren't a feminist. In a way, feminism is making your own choices, and not being told you can't do something.

ST: But not with anger. That's the part I like to leave out. You can be strong and independent. But for some reason, I feel that when you say "feminist" there's an extremity to it. I don't want to be associated with that negative side of it. I really feel that the beauty of the differences of the sexes is the *difference*. That's the beauty. That's what's so nice about it. We don't want a generic society. That's what's so beautiful about the different cultures. They're very significant to our survival. We need to appreciate our differences.

BH: Otherwise life would be awfully boring.

ST: I love men. I love my husband. I appreciate everything that men represent. But at the same time, I feel that we as women also have something very beautiful. We represent a lot of great things that we just haven't been recognized for before. I think that we should be recognized and appreciated for all of the things we bring to life. Not being taken for granted. That's all.

BH: Some of your songs are so appealing in a breezy, light-hearted way, but they make a point. I think a lot of women are empowered by some of your songs. Not in a feminist way, but because the song makes them see a situation differently. Songs have so much power in society.

ST: People live their lives by music; I believe that.

BH: I think that you can hear a song and you can change your mind about something.

ST: It's no different than poetry. We are very much influenced by what we read. It's very true. You're a writer; you influence a lot of people, I'm very sure. Songs can solidify what you are already thinking. Or maybe you're on the fence, a lot of times, and a song can make a difference.

BH: You make your points in a fun, musical way.

ST: With the songs that we have on this album [*The Woman in Me*], I think they make couples chuckle at each other, as opposed to being angry with each other. You can have a sense of humor about making your point. That's really our approach.

BH: You're also bringing romance back into people's lives through your music.

ST: I miss that. I like romance. I love all those things. The thing for me is to get the most out of life. That means in every way. That means in a professional way. That means in a romantic way. That means in a feminine way. There are a lot of different sides to women. We can do a lot of men's jobs. I don't believe necessarily that we can do all men's jobs, and I don't believe that they can do all our jobs. But I think, of all the things that as a human being, whether you're a woman or not, that you can do, the better for you. The more well-rounded, the more complete your life is going to be. And romance definitely has to be one of them. You can't just be a hard-assed woman who's out there kicking butt. I think you're missing something if you're not enjoying the romance that life has to offer, and the feminine side of what we have to offer. I never like to get too far away from that in my music.

BH: You don't have to be in a new relationship. You can be well into a relationship and you still need romance.

ST: You need it more.

BH: About your writing. How do you write your songs?

ST: Sometimes I come up with a melody when we're in the car, and if I didn't bring the tape deck, I have to sing it all the way home so I don't forget it. Then when I get home I run up to the tape deck to record it. We write everywhere. When we're driving to the grocery store, we write. Or my husband might be watching hockey or something in the living room, and I'll be in the kitchen cooking dinner, and we'll be writing a song at the same time. We're so old-fashioned that way. I love to be in the kitchen and he loves to watch sports. . . .

BH: With both of you in the music business, and being creative, it must be fabulous.

ST: It's great. The thing about music, it's part of your lifestyle. It's not work. We have that in common. But, look, he's the producer. I don't go into the studio to tweak the guitar sound for ten hours. I can't even be interested in that. I know what sound I want. I can tell him creatively what I want. We don't have those things in common. And he doesn't do my thing. He doesn't go out and do interviews.

BH: Mutt doesn't even have a public persona. He seems very much a recluse.

ST: He doesn't want to be a celebrity. He isn't that type of person. We are very different people at the same time as having something that's very much in common. The amazing part of it is creating the writing part that we share together. We don't even consider it work. When we're writing, we're having fun. We might be in the canoe, or we might be going to get groceries, or we might be taking a walk. When we're on a vacation, that's when we get so much writing done. And we don't consider it work.

BH: That's one way to keep your marriage strong.

ST: It's wonderful.

BH: You've talked about your mom and dad running a company together. In a lot of ways, it doesn't matter if you're running a tree-planting company or creating music, the more you can share in your life together . . .

ST: . . . the closer you get.

BH: You talked about wanting to run away to Africa, and you actually got to go to Africa recently—to Egypt to shoot one of your videos.

ST: I've been to Africa since, too. I went to Johannesburg, South Africa, because my husband's family lives there. But I did go to Egypt, like you were saying, to make a video. That was a great experience.

BH: I was in Cairo once for a few days, and one of the memories I have is this cart with a horse and in the back of the cart were all these watermelons. The horse had this bucket on its face, and he was walking down the street eating his oats. Or maybe it was a donkey.

ST: I bet it was a donkey. And they pull ten times their weight.

BH: There were hundreds of watermelons.

ST: I don't know how they do it.

BH: Do you want to perform all over the world, once you starting touring?

ST: I want to be as international as possible.

BH: Right now, is your record in Europe?

ST: It is in Europe, but it's just getting started there. But, I get fan mail from Japan. I get fan mail from Australia. I get fan mail from England.

BH: But your biggest fans are Canadians. They have to be.

ST: My most loyal fans, I'm sure.

BH: You have become part of the pop culture in Canada so quickly, it's amazing. Everyone seems to know who you are up north.

ST: I'm not even aware of it. I have no idea.

BH: My travel agent was so excited when I told him I was going to L.A. to interview you. He even asked me to bring back a photograph of you. And I know of this fifteen-year-old girl who's doing a social studies paper about you at school. She found a Shania Twain home page on the Internet and printed copies of all your lyrics and biography for her report. Just last month, I was on a reserve in a remote part of British Columbia, and the teenaged girls I was doing a workshop with are just crazy about you.

ST: That's great.

BH: I saw you a year ago when you performed in Vancouver at the National Aboriginal Achievement Awards, and you weren't that well-known then. Except maybe to die-hard country fans.

ST: It's happened very quickly.

BH: What are your plans for your next album? Are you working on one right now?

ST: We're actually just getting started with the writing. Over the next few months I think we'll accomplish a great deal with the songwriting. Then we'll go in the studio and we'll record it and we'll experiment with it. I'm sure that by the fall we'll be finished with the album.

BH: You want to release an album before you go on tour?

ST: The album will be out before I tour.

BH: Your current album, *The Woman in Me*, seems to have a life that won't end. You listen to most albums and you might hear three hits. But with your album, almost every song sounds like it could be a radio hit. Last night you performed "No One Needs to Know" on the *Tonight Show with Jay Leno*. I didn't even know that you were releasing it as a single. Just when you think the last single has been released, another one comes out.

ST: You'd like to think that the album's life will be at least a year or more, or the amount of time that you put into it. The same will go for the next album. We've been working on songs for the next album since this album came out. It's an ongoing process. That's why we've got such a great start on songs for the next album. For the past year or more, we've been working on the next album. It's a long, slow process.

BH: You perform with a live band on television talk shows and at awards shows. Do you have a regular band or do you use studio musicians when you perform?

ST: I piece the band together for performances right now.

BH: I have to ask you this question—what kind of horses do you own? I rode horses growing up, and now my oldest daughter is starting to ride. She started taking English lessons when she was six. She is such a horse fan.

ST: I'm just getting started again with horses. I was around horses when I was younger and I've always wanted to have horses of my own. I've handled horses before, so I feel comfortable, but I still need time to get reintroduced. We have two quarter horses right now—one's a palomino, and the other one is a paint. They're well-trained. Now I'm looking into maybe a Tennessee walking horse.

BH: I've ridden Tennessee walkers. They have this wonderful gait. It feels like you're on this cushion when you're riding them.

ST: We ride cross-country, because we're out in the bush, so they'd be great for us.

BH: You can ride a Tennessee walker for miles and not get tired. They have a really smooth trot.

ST: Some quarter horses can have a really rough trot. So I am considering a Tennessee walker.

BH: I know you've got a lot of interviews set up today. Do you want to keep going, or do you want to take a break, or have some time to yourself?

ST: I'm fine; I don't need a break.

BH: You're like an Eveready battery. . . .

ST: When I'm in that mode, I can just keep going.

BH: The book that I'm writing is about Aboriginal Canadians, and I'd like to talk a bit about how your Aboriginal heritage has affected you.

ST: I have met non-Native people who, for some reason, want to be Native. They want the spirituality; they want to braid their hair. I don't get it. I want to say to them, Listen, you try to be raised North American Indian in this country. Do you realize the reality and burden that comes along with it? Like I was saying to you, there's no way, after being raised the way we were raised, that I'm going to be stripped of that now. This is already my reality. I've weathered the good and the bad, and I want to keep the good and the bad.

Being Native is not only about the spiritual experience. That's something that Native communities are regaining, that they're educating themselves about. But I can guarantee you that the typical Native community in Canada, at least the ones I know, they're like everybody else, except they're standing in quicksand.

BH: We eat cornflakes, we watch TV, we go to McDonald's. Recovering our languages and cultures is part of it too.

ST: It's what we're fighting to preserve and regain. That's almost, right now, still at an intellectual stage. It takes generations. Even my grandparents have lost some of their traditions. My grandparents were raised on reservations. My father was for a while. They've got wonderful stories about how they lived their life on a daily basis in the north. The reality of being Native in Canada is how you live your everyday life, whether that means in a traditional way, or by using your language, or simply surviving.

BH: People tend to romanticize Native life. It isn't like we sit around all winter doing bead work and holding ceremonies, although that may be part of some Aboriginal peoples' lives, even today.

ST: It's about practical, everyday life. And even though everyday life has evolved and changed, there are traditional ways that we want to hold on to, that we want to preserve.

BH: Being in touch with your history, your heritage, gives you a richer and fuller life. The schools have to be involved in teaching that. It's a whole process of being reeducated about our cultures, because we've lost a lot of that over the past century or two.

ST: I don't like to talk to the media about growing up in a Native family, because people tend to romanticize it. Some people want me to have grown up with braids and feathers in my hair. That isn't what we did. We grew up like every other family in Canada, but there were things that definitely made our family different from our white neighbors. There's no doubt about it.

BH: I think you've handled this controversy [about your heritage] extremely well. I think the only people you have to answer to about your family history is your family.

ST: We all live in the same world. We're all going through the same political problems as a country, as a planet. We all have to go through it together. The distinction comes in your heart. And you either pursue it or you don't. I choose to hang on to whatever it is that I've had in my past.

BH: You've got a strong sense of identity, of family. If you keep getting this media backlash about your heritage, you just have to remember that you have a total sense of where you've come from.

ST: It's just such a reality to me that it doesn't even matter. There's no way that anyone is going to get an inconsistent answer from me [about my Native heritage].

BH: It looks like your next interviewer is here. It was great meeting and talking to you, Shania. Good luck tomorrow at the Academy of Country Music Awards.

ST: Thank you for coming by today.